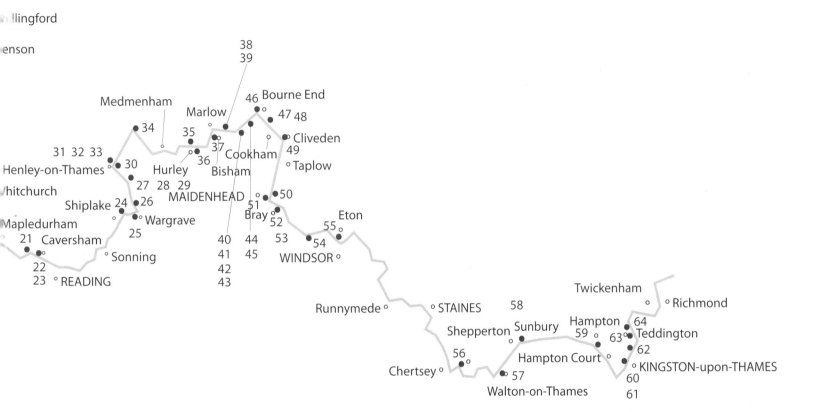

allingford

enson

38
39

Medmenham
Marlow
46 Bourne End
47 48
34
35
Cliveden
31 32 33
30
37
49
Cookham
Henley-on-Thames
Hurley
36
Taplow
Bisham
27 28 29
Whitchurch
MAIDENHEAD
Shiplake 24
26
50
Mapledurham
25 Wargrave
51
Bray 52
Eton
21 Caversham
55
40
44 53
54
22
41 45
Sonning
42 WINDSOR
23 ° READING
43

Twickenham
Richmond
Runnymede ° STAINES 58
Hampton 64
Teddington
Shepperton Sunbury 59 63 62
56 Hampton Court KINGSTON-upon-THAMES
Chertsey 57 60
Walton-on-Thames 61

41 Clay-hung   51 'Spooky'   61 Cream Swiss Chalet
42 Dragon   52 Green Mesh   62 Royal Canoe
43 Aqua Trellis   53 Contemporary spire   63 Aldous
44 White Boathouse   54 Oakley Court   64 Teddington
45 Noah's   55 Eton
46 Upper Thames Sailing Club   56 Weybridge Mariners
47 Barn   57 Thameside Boathouse Terrace
48 Cookham neo-Tudor   58 Sentinel
49 Cliveden   59 Hucks'
50 Timber and tin   60 Ruskinian Gothic

Boathouses

Boathouses

Clare Sherriff

Unicorn Press

For Katy Clemson
Artist and Printmaker

Unicorn Press
76 Great Suffolk Street
London SE1 0BL

email: unicornpress@btinternet.com
www.unicornpress.org

First published by Unicorn Press 2008

ISBN 978 0906290 97 2

Designed by Karen Wilks
Printed in China by 1010 Printing International Limited

frontispiece: **Inside the Trevarno Boathouse near Helston, Cornwall**
Robert Down Photographers Direct 2006

Contents

The Harbour Control Tower, Lisbon
KME Germany AG 2001
The three bays of boat storage are at the base of the building

My aim in this book has been to bring together and illustrate for comparison a selection of boathouses from around the world. In the British Isles a journey down the non-tidal part of the river Thames, between Lechlade and Teddington, reveals an eclectic mix of history and design, both in contemporary boathouse building and in the more traditional late-nineteenth- and early-twentieth-century prototypes. To complete the picture I have also included some notable boathouses on the shores of Britain's lochs, lakes and rivers. The boathouses illustrated are private and institutional, or in a few cases commercial.

A boathouse is a utilitarian building, rather like a garage; its purpose is to house and shelter boats. A boathouse is built either as an independent structure, or as an internal dock within a house or building. The term boathouse covers both in the book. Boathouses are distinguished by being either wet, where water flows into a dock, or dry for storing lighter craft, or sometimes they are a combination of the two. But quite unlike the design history of the garage, boats and water seem to have inspired owners and architects to introduce a note of theatre, even fantasy and glamour into their designs, which can be particularly eye-catching. Whether built for business or pleasure, there is no doubt that boathouses continue to provide design opportunities for their owners and builders which are denied to 'land-lubbers'. With shelter for boats come the leisure needs and desires of owners and visitors for accommodation, so more sophisticated boathouses, with bedrooms, living rooms and verandas are designed. This creates more scope for introducing the quirky, eccentric and fun into their buildings.

Today boathouses cross the line between utility and eccentricity – fishermen use them as a working base, lifeboat men launch their rescue missions from them, writers and poets have found refuge and inspiration in them, in Japan a whole community lives in a boathouse village, children boat from them in our parks and wealthy landowners use them as play-stations on their estates. They inspire community projects, holiday homes, iconic university buildings, working facilities and design competitions. Wood is a common denominator, utility a dictator and luxury often the licence for boathouse design.

Boathouses also cross the boundaries of form. Although examples chosen range from the simple, rustic and tumble-down to the very grand or the ultra streamlined contemporary; from the 'A' frame to the multi-gabled or even castellated, from the basic barn to the sophisticated steel and glass structure, it seems both form and fancy have their place. The influence of Britain as an empire and trading nation in the nineteenth century had a notable influence on architecture in former colonies across the world; this is true also of boathouse design.

Boathouses are unique in that they combine two essential elements, land and water. A boathouse seems the ultimate retreat for the escapist – alluring and romantic. The philosopher, Alain de Botton, writes about 'the...tension between order and chaos' in architecture. Water, even at its most tame, holds elements of danger; the juxtaposition of building right on the edge of water electrifies the architectural experience.[1] The opportunity to construct a boathouse creates a blend of landscape with water, a special light and sympathetic materials. Structurally it is challenging to meet the distinctive needs of water and weather resistance; changes in the environment make ever-increasing demands on choices of site, materials and construction methods. With eco-sustainability an important issue in architecture today, and the trend for architecture with computer-led design to assume previously unimagined shapes, the boathouse in its traditional and new-found forms has interesting potential as a building type.

I hope that there will be something here to stimulate discussion between owners, potential owners, builders, planners and architects – and between those, like many of us, who may dream about the fantasy of building a boathouse of our own.

Chapter 1 : Boathouses around the World

Contemporary architects worldwide are embracing the dynamics of new boathouse commissions. The architectural practice of PLOT in Copenhagen innovatively designed one of the most appealing new boathouses of this century – one which combines the use of a youth centre and a boathouse store for around fifty boats, built in a former industrial district south of Copenhagen. PLOT was founded in Copenhagen in 2001 by the architects Bjarke Ingels and Julien De Smedt, with a design philosophy to create a narrative within a building, 'a series of events that are tied together in a PLOT'.[2] Their clients 'desires were opposite...the sail club needed most of the site to park their boats' and the children's requirements were for meeting and extensive play areas. PLOT's solution was an undulating hardwood deck allowing 'for boat storage underneath, still letting the kids run/play above... The actual room of the Maritime Youth House IS the wooden deck' – a paradise for skate boarders or rolling bodies, and seemingly for sailors alike.[3]

The wave-like movement of the decks makes a natural connection between children and the sea – both concept and design are self-enhancing. The building is simply a synthesis of community and leisure needs. The Maritime Youth Centre has, by thinking round the PLOT, created an unusual and simple solution.

opposite: **Interior of Peter Jay Sharp Boathouse, Swindler's Cove**
Armand Le Gardeur with Peter Aaron/Esto 2004

1.1 and 1.2 The Maritime Youth House Amager, Copenhagen
PLOT Architects Paolo Roselli 2004

1.3 The Maritime Youth House Amager, Copenhagen
Mads Hilmer 2004

1.4 Rolling Kids, The Maritime Youth House Amager, Copenhagen
2004

1.5 Multi-purpose Room
The Maritime Youth House Amager, Copenhagen
Julien de Smedt 2004

1.6 Winning Design for Alvar Aalto's Boathouse
Maija Holma Alvar Aalto Museum 1998

Five years earlier, two Danish architecture students, Claudia Schulz and Anne-Mette Krolmark, won a design competition for a boat shed to house the Finnish designer Alvar Aalto's boat, *'Nemo propheta in Patria'* at his summer house in Muuratsalo, central Finland.[4] The competition was organised by the Alvar Aalto Museum, the School of Architecture in Helsinki and the local authorities. The lateral simplicity of the timbers, contrasting with the strong verticals of the woodland setting, echo Aalto's deep affinity with the quiet forests of his native Finland, and his search for buildings to rest organically within their landscape. 'Architecture must be deeply rooted in place and circumstance...; it must support man's emotional life,' he told an audience in a speech honouring his fellow architect, Eliel Saarinen.[5] Aalto's boat shelter makes a consummate integration of his design philosophy within its woodland habitat.

The countries of Norway and Sweden reveal an interesting phenomenon in boathouse design – their boathouses, often found in clusters, are generally simple, barn-like structures. Nearly all are painted a distinctive russet red – derived from copper ore – giving them strong national identity. Corners and barge-boarding are traditionally painted white.

Northern Europe has a strong sea-faring tradition and it is not surprisingly home to innovative boathouse building. The 'A' frame and fresh patchwork colours of this Icelandic camp of fisherman's boathouses create another indigenous type, though not necessarily typical of the country. They were probably built in the late 1940s, and are made of corrugated iron. Originally they were painted green, but are now an assortment of blues and sugar almond colours, which in a cold landscape, should cheer up anyone's day.

1.7 Bud Boathouses, Norway
Sue Keane 2006

overleaf: **1.8 The Icelandic Patchwork Boathouses, Hafnarfjord, Nr Reykjavik**
Konrad Ragnarsson Photographers Direct 2007

1.9 Lake Königssee Boathouses
Antonina Ivasenko Photographers Direct 2007

1.10 Lake Lugano Boathouse
Lisa Engelbrecht www.Danitadelimont.com 2006

The boathouses on the alpine Lake Königssee in Germany lie deep in the Berchtesgaden National Park, below the famous Watzmann Mountain. The lake's emerald green water is legendary. The lake is also famous for the pilgrim church of St Bartholomä, and for the boathouses in Schönau, with their distinctive hipped roofs. Respect for the environment of the lake was a concern even in 1909, when 'electromotor' boats were introduced. These 'slender' wooden boats are unique to the region. Today only rowing boats and the electromotors are allowed, making Lake Königssee 'one of the cleanest lakes in Germany'. The boathouses are probably contemporary with the boats, built in the early twentieth century.[6]

Reflected in the quiet waters of Lake Lugano, this simple building with its off-centre arched boat storage, shuttered windows, faded stucco and roman tiled roof has intense appeal.

1.11 The Lisbon Harbour Control Tower
KME Germany AG 2001

The Harbour Control Tower in Lisbon was built at a seemingly precarious angle by the Portuguese architect Gonçalo Sousa Byrne in 2001. It has nine storeys, clad in copper sheets with a glass box on top, giving the impression of a lighthouse. The ground-floor plinth contains the entrance and three bays of boat storage.

The pointed stone arches of the Seljuk boathouses in Turkey form the entrance to the shipyard of the ancient castle of Seljuk. Romans, Byzantines and Seljuks have all played a part in its construction. A six-kilometre wall and one hundred and forty watch towers protect the castle itself. The shipyard has five docks and was built in 1226 by the Sultan Alaaddin Keykubat. Internally each bay is linked by equilateral arches. The complex, built into the cliff of the Turkish coast line, contains offices and a small mosque to the left of the entrance.

This fisherman's dry stone boatshed, on a small bay at the southern side of the Greek island of Samos, shows that even the most run-down shelter can still be effective...nearly...

1.14 The Art Deco Boathouse, Sanganer, Jaipur State, India (1936-40)

C. J. Parker RIBA Photographs Collection

In India, with its lineage of lake palaces and legendary wealth of the Maharajahs, it is not surprising that this crisp Art Deco boathouse, with its distinctive rounded lines, was built in the 1930s in Jaipur, as a statement of modernity. It is believed that the architect, Cecil James Parker (1906-72), worked for the firm of William Wood and Partners. Their portfolio included factories and offices in Malaya, South Africa and Singapore and in the UK, the Marconi Building in Chelmsford built in the 1930s.

In Japan, as in India and Thailand, whole communities live on the water. One such area in Japan has around four hundred 'Funaya' or boathouses. The Ine-ura district in the town of Ine-cho, situated in the north-eastern tip of the Tango Peninsula, in the Kyoto Prefecture, was made a preservation area in 2005. Boathouses in this district are 'residential houses built on the water's edge with their ground floors used [for] accommodating boats.' 'The recent enlargement of fishing vessels has prompted house dwellers to remodel boathouses and turn them into their living rooms or party rooms for private lodging' and for tourism.[7] The older boathouses were built at the end of the Edo period (1603-1867) and the newer ones in the early Showa period (1926-45).

On the Bassac River near Phnom Penh, on the Mekong Delta in Cambodia a similar fishing village grew up about ten years ago. Floating villages in this region tend to be established by Vietnamese communities looking to create a livelihood. The boats are moored alongside the living quarters; monsoon conditions and severe poverty provide little opportunity for boathouse building.

An eighteenth-century lithograph by Louis Leborne (1796-1863) shows a boat hanger built for the chief Palou of the Tonga-Tabou tribe. A French expedition during the years 1826-1829 aboard the *L'Astrolabe* resulted in the crew meeting the people and chief Palou in Tonga, in the South Pacific. The history of the expedition was published later.[8] The shape of the boat hanger is reminiscent of the upturned prow of a boat. It seems a natural and inspired solution for boat storage.

overleaf: **1.16 Vue d'un hangar abritant la pirogue de guerre du chef Palou, Tonga-Tabou, 1833**
Louis Leborne (1796-1865), National Library of Australia

1.17 Boatsheds on Watercress, Paterson Inlet, Stewart Island, New Zealand

Neil Rawlins Photographers Direct 2004

1.18 The Melbourne University Rowing Club

Katy Lefroy 2008

Simple beach boathouses are indigenous to both Australia and New Zealand; they are often found grouped together, in much the same way as a row of beach huts are found in English seaside towns. These boat sheds at Watercress on Paterson Inlet, Stewart Island, New Zealand form an irregular line of wooden huts on stilts. Neil Rawlins, a travel writer and photographer, writes that Stewart Island is the third island of New Zealand, with less than three hundred residents. These numbers swell in the summer, when tourists brave a sometimes choppy passage from South Island. Fishing and dependence on boats has always been a way of life on Stewart Island. The boatsheds are used by locals and also 'off-islanders' to store small craft. Some have been modified; here the middle shed has had a balcony and additional room added in recent years, presumably with the hope of making it into the dream island retreat.

Melbourne University Boathouse, belonging to the oldest rowing club in Australia, is an altogether grander example of boathouse building. This is a fine example of a colonial boathouse, but with a particular distinction. The traditional gable format is enhanced by its round-arched balcony, belvedere-like tower, and boathouse storage below.

1.19 The Club de Regatas La Marina, Tigre, Argentina

Harriet Cummings Photographers Direct 2007

opposite: **1.20 Boldt Castle Yacht House**

Neil Koven Photographers Direct 2004

Staying in the southern hemisphere, but moving to the opposite side of the world, the Club de Regatas La Marina – CRLM – in the city of Tigre, twenty miles from Buenos Aires in Argentina is a building of impressive stature and proportions for a rowing club. Tigre is home to a colony of boat clubs built in a variety of styles ranging from the neo-Tudor to the Venetian Gothic, Dutch Renaissance and Crenellated Ecclesiastical. The CRLM, built in 1927, adds a new twist to this collection, merging neo-Tudor with the Spanish Hacienda. Tigre is known as 'Argentina's Henley', and has the buildings to prove it. The CRLM is a rectangular building whose central section, crowned by an exuberant cupola, dominates the scene. Half-timbering, extensive balconies and a mass of fenestration, combine with an impressive arcade of ground floor bays, distinguished by their shallow segmental arches. The central arch is the gateway into the vast boathouse behind.

In Canada on Wellesley Island, in the St Lawrence River, the timbered Bavarian fantasy of Boldt Castle, with its massive tripartite boathouse, was built to house the Boldt family's three yachts, which included an 'enormous' houseboat. Its grandiose scale defies even the most egotistical of builders. George Boldt emigrated to America from Prussia in 1864 and began his career in the hotel business, rising to become manager of the Waldorf-Astoria in New York. He later bought the Bellevue-Stratford Hotel in Philadelphia, and was acknowledged as one of the leading hoteliers of his day. The Boldt Yacht House, completed in 1904, was built to reflect the design of the castle, with towers, spires and steeply-pitched gables. It contains three yacht bays, a service bay, and a crenellated tower, alongside crew and staff quarters. The building is now the property of the Thousand Islands' Bridge Authority and is listed on the National Register of Historic Places. It is open to the public.[9]

1.21 Bending Birches Boathouse, The Rideau

Ken Watson Photographers Direct 2002

1.22 Murphy Bay Boathouse, Rideau Lake

Ken Watson Photographers Direct 2002

1.23 Driftwood, Lake Rosseau
John De Visser 2006

Canada has a strong boathouse tradition. The Big Rideau Lake in Ontario is a UNESCO World Heritage Site and is home to some highly distinctive boathouses. The Rideau is a 202-kilometre-long waterway which links Kingston, Ontario to Ottawa in the north. Kingston was a British naval base when the Rideau was first opened in 1832. The Rideau is the oldest continuously operated canal in North America. By the end of the nineteenth century the Rideau's commercial use was declining, and the area was used more for recreation. Today the Rideau is operated as a recreational waterway by Parks Canada, an agency of the Canadian government. Bending Birches Boathouses are roughly twenty-five years old, having replaced a single older boathouse. Their bleached wood and gaunt simplicity are striking. They have the traditional boathouse shape of a gabled roof and open water bays, with a lean-to addition and cantilevered bay.

This Rideau Lake boathouse shows the more traditional American boathouse clap-board genre with hipped gable, deep eaves, balcony, boathouse bays and surrounding decks. It has decorative fretwork on the gables and is a typical example of the high standard of boathouse building in America.[10]

The Driftwood boathouse is located on Lake Rosseau, one of the three lakes that make up the 'Muskoka' region, comprising Lake Muskoka, Lake Rosseau and Lake Joseph, covering around 680-790 square kilometres, north of Toronto. Driftwood, the Deluce family boathouse, was built in 1988 with a distinctive roofline of gables, rounded dormer windows and 'belfry' spirelets. Its many 'window shapes' are 'the trademark of architect Tony Marsh'. The boathouse has three boat slips, two covered boat 'ports' and 'a specially designed dock for Bob Deluce's Cessna 185 float plane'. Its design apparently draws reference to 'the grey-shingled seaside houses built along the New England coast in the late 1800s'.[11] This is a fairy-tale boathouse, synthesising glamour and function, reflecting the skills of Canadian boathouse building.

1.24 The Peter Jay Sharp Boathouse, Swindler's Cove
Armand Le Gardeur with Peter Aaron/Esto 2004

1.25 Interior of Peter Jay Sharp Boathouse, Swindler's Cove
Armand Le Gardeur with Peter Aaron/Esto 2004

Following the American clap-board tradition, the Canadian company, International Marine Floatation Systems, is producing some interesting boathouse designs. Whilst the greater part of their portfolio is for floating houses, they built the Peter Jay Sharp Boathouse at Swindler's Cove on the Harlem River on New York's waterfront. This is the first new community boathouse in New York City in nearly one hundred years, and is part of the New York Restoration Project – NYRP – and also home to the New York Rowing Association. It is the only existing floating boathouse on the East Coast. Its design was inspired by the nineteenth- and early-twentieth-century boathouses on this section of the river, which was locally known as 'Sculler's Row'. The building has extensive boat storage for racing shells, locker rooms, an exercise room with rowing machines, and generous viewing platforms. The firm of Robert A.M. Stern Architects oversaw the design stage of the project which was spearheaded by the singer Bette Midler, founder of NYRP, in an effort to restore public access to the waterfront. Her dream was to provide a safe place where local kids could learn to row, whilst restoring an area spoilt by industrial waste – Swindler Cove Park was built on a former illegal dumping ground. In addition to the Peter Jay Sharp Foundation, other charitable trusts and the New York State Office of Parks, Recreation and Historic Preservation, individual donors such as Bette Midler and Yoko Ono made contributions to the project. IMF designed and built the float in Vancouver and it was trucked to New Jersey for assembly and construction. The building has deep eaves, generous fenestration and balconies and is much enhanced by its vibrant colour scheme.

1.26 The Gilder Boathouse, Yale University USA

Turner Brooks Architects Eeva Pelkonen and Michael Curtis
Michael Marsland 2002

1.27 The Model

Turner Brooks Architects Eeva Pelkonen and Michael Curtis

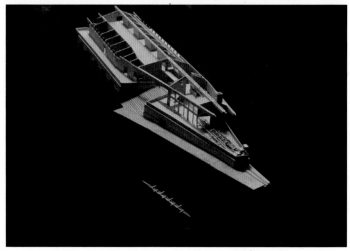

1.28 The Gilder Boathouse, Yale University, USA
Elevation and Floor Plans, showing boat storage on the lower level,
rowers and staff facilities and the Viewing Room
Turner Brooks Architects Eeva Pelkonen and Michael Curtis

The American firm of Turner Brooks Architects was commissioned to build the Gilder Boathouse for Yale University in 1998 and completed it in 2000 at a cost of 5.5 million dollars. Rowing has been a part of the Yale scene since the mid-nineteenth century. The new boathouse is a state-of-the-art rowing facility, sited at the finishing line of the university's 2,000-metre race course on the Housatonic River.

The architect Turner Brooks describes the building:
'The main building entrance brings athletes, coaches and visitors through the heraldic sliding oar "door" (a clustered frieze of aluminium oars) into a porch that opens up dramatically to a framed view of the river. Here a generously expanding stair spills down to connect with the docks and the water below. The staircase and deck function as a multipurpose space for team meetings and other group activities...A lounge is located south of the river for viewing the approach of racing boats. This space, anchored by a large fireplace, is also designed to house trophies and other memorabilia.' [12]

An aerial view of the model of the building instantly suggests its nautical inspiration. The upturned prow of Chief Palou Tonga-Tabou's early boat shelter was conceived with a similar nautical form in mind. The dockside view of the building shows the terraces, the main Viewing Room and the boat ramps with storage below. The low profile sits well on the water, giving reference to its aquatic status. The overhanging platform commands the view, like the bridge of an ocean liner. The diagonals of the boat ramp walkway connect the parking and trailer storage areas to the dock area below. The Viewing Room is a triumph of cedar wood and glass, and is much complemented by bespoke furniture, designed by Turner Brooks.[13]

SOUTH SECTION / ELEVATION

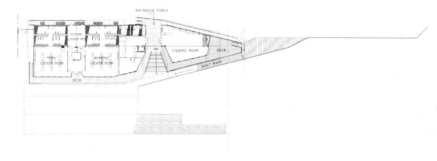

UPPER LEVEL PLAN

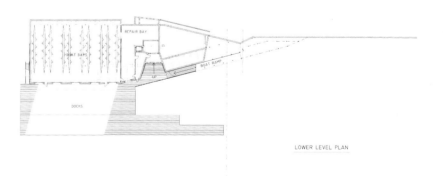

LOWER LEVEL PLAN

1.29 The Gilder Boathouse, looking up the stairs from the docks
Turner Brooks Architects Eeva Pelkonen and Michael Curtis
Richard Cadan 2006

1.30 The Gilder Boathouse, Yale University, USA
The Viewing Room
Turner Brooks Architects Eeva Pelkonen and Michael Curtis
2006

The designs of boathouses, whether nautically inspired, fantastical or simple clap-boarded seem to reach out to public imagination. Boathouse Row at Schuylkill River, Fairmont Park in Pennsylvania is illuminated at night and is a major tourist attraction in the area. Its gabled profiles and boathouse entrances make a captivating lighted spectacle. The Canadian lakes similarly contain a number of sumptuous boathouses, built to exacting standards, which individually and collectively have immense appeal.

This selection of boathouses from around the world can do no more than introduce and provide an opportunity to compare the main categories: the 'A' frame, the barn or agrarian building, the gabled colonial boathouse with balcony and fretwork, the simple beach hut or clap-board boathouse, the boathouse terrace and now the post-modern boathouse, endowed with space, light and innovative use of materials. The new generation of architect-designed boathouses elevates the building type, taking it into the realm of world-class architecture.

Chapter 2 : The British Boathouse

The British Isles is home to an intriguing range of boathouses, many of which deserve to be in this chapter. The examples chosen to represent the British Isles illustrate a range of eye-catching design from Classic to Gothic, including boathouses with rustic origins, or those with strong literary connections, or simply boathouses with grand stories to tell.

The Trevarno Boathouse near Helston in Cornwall is perhaps, one of the most picturesque in England. It was built for William Bickford-Smith c. 1870s, and is believed to be the only timber-framed boathouse of its period in Cornwall. It sits on the edge of a landscaped lake, surrounded by an estate of mature trees and shrubs. Its simple wooden structure is decorated with trefoil lattice-glazed windows and ornate barge-boards, clay ridge tiles and a tiered 'belfry' cupola, which emphasises the ecclesiastical theme. This is the Victorian Gothic in vernacular mode.

2.2 The Trevarno Boathouse
Robert Down Photographers Direct 2006

opposite: **2.1 Inside the Trevarno Boathouse**
Robert Down Photographers Direct 2006

Greenway Boathouse on the banks of the River Dart in Devon has Tudor connections, rustic origins, and a strong literary connection. Greenway is often referred to locally as 'Raleigh's Boathouse'. Walter Raleigh – Elizabeth I's pirate buccaneer – was half-brother to Sir John Gilbert, a local landowner. The National Trust, who own the property, suggest that 'it is possible that a structure stood here during his lifetime and that he could have [used] it due to…family connections on his mother's side;' this is however unproven. The Greenway boathouse is a simple, single-storey, stone structure, sitting on a rock shelf, with a steep slipway to the river. An internal doorway (now blocked-up) leads to the bathing room, which it is believed dates from the late eighteenth century. By 1839 the boathouse is recorded as having a 'plunge pool' so that family and guests at Greenway could 'take the tidal salt waters of the Dart' in safety. This transports the idea of the Victorian seaside bathing hut to the river; a private plunge pool was an unusual feature for a house at that time. The pool is roughly 5m by 4m, with a height of 1.8m; the flow of water from the river in and out of the pool 'is controlled by a sluice rod adjacent to the steps'.[14] On the first floor is the main room of the boathouse, lit by three round-arched windows, a fanlight and a generous balcony. This is a wide room full of light, warmed by a Victorian fireplace, which is decorated with blue and white Delft tiles. In the twentieth century Greenway was home to the 'Queen' of crime writers, Agatha Christie; travel up the Dart on a boat and you will undoubtedly be told that this was Agatha Christie's boathouse, a building which 'nestled remote in its trees with its little balcony and its small quay below'.[15] It was here that the fictional Marlene Tucker was strangled in *Dead Man's Folly*.

Boathouses are often found in lonely, very beautiful locations. It is no wonder that writers and painters are drawn to such surroundings. The Welsh poet Dylan Thomas found inspiration in his Laugharne Boathouse on the Carmarthenshire coast, where he wrote *Under Milk Wood*. Dylan and his wife, Caitlin, had always dreamed of living in the boathouse. They arrived in Laugharne in 1949. He adopted the shed close to the boathouse, 'his water and tree room,' as his writing retreat. The walls were covered with photographs and writings of his favourite authors, Byron, Auden, Walt Whitman and William Blake. His view of the Tâf estuary was one of wholesale beauty and peace. The boathouse included a first-floor parlour and bedroom for their oldest child, Llewelyn. The top floor had further bedrooms for Dylan and his wife and their other two children, whilst the kitchen and sitting room were in the basement. The house was 'notoriously cold and damp' and had no electricity or running water, until improvements were made. Such discomforts were immaterial, the light, the views and the silence made Dylan observe that 'there is nowhere else like the Boat House'.[16]

'This tumbling house whose every broken pane and wind-whipped-off slate, childscrawled wall, rain-stain mousehole, knobble and ricket, man-bobby and rat-trap, I know in my sleep,' was his natural habitat, etched deep inside his soul.[17]

Dylan Thomas' boathouse is now in the care of Carmarthenshire County Council and is open to the public.

2.5 Inside Dylan Thomas's Writing Shed by the Boathouse, Laugharne

Geoff Charles 1955 by permission of Llyfrgell Genedlaethol Cymru/The National Library of Wales

2.6 The Dougarie Boathouse, Isle of Arran
Lavinia Gibbs 2005

2.7 Dougarie Boathouse Interior, Isle of Arran
Country Life August 8th 1996

The Dougarie Boathouse on the Isle of Arran in Scotland is as poetic a setting as that of Laugharne. It was built for William, 12th Duke of Hamilton, of local Arran sandstone, and was completed in 1885. Two boathouses are joined by a central section, of two stepped saddles, with a rustic columned veranda below.[18] Most distinctive are the narrow gables and splayed rooflines, giving the building an almost Chinese look. The central room of the boathouse was used for games and entertaining; cartoons decorate the walls, depicting local characters. An article by Jeremy Musson in *Country Life* explains that the majority of these were drawn by an Italian artist, Liberio Prosperi, 'a cartoonist for *Vanity Fair* from the 1860s to 1890s.'[19] It is thought that the boathouse is the work of the architect John James Burnet (1857-1938) of Burnet and Campbell, but this is unproven. Burnet had a number of commissions for the 12th Duke of Hamilton on the island at the time. His fame was established when he built the King Edward VII Galleries at the British Museum in 1903. Thomas Weir, a civil engineer from Glasgow, was responsible for the foundations and slipway of the boathouse and Robert McAuley of Glasgow constructed the timber-work.[20]

The Rosehaugh Boathouse in Ross-shire was built in the 1900s by the Victorian architect William Flockhart (1854-1913) for James Douglas Fletcher, whose family fortune was made in the alpaca trade in the early nineteenth century. Included in the extensive programme of works was 'a plan to dam the stream in a valley in the Estate grounds, to create a sporting lake and also to generate sufficient water pressure to power turbines to generate electricity for the house. The boathouse was built on the shore of the lake, timber-framed on a base of rough random stone, with a pitched roof covered with pink tiles. A high-level balcony...extended along three sides of the upper floor. At the water level were the slipways, moorings and undercover boat storage, while the room upstairs was well lit, with a luxuriously furnished lounge and handsome stone fireplace. [The boathouse] was accessible by a bridge from the hill behind the building, onto the upper balcony'. The dam gave way in the mid 1940s and the boathouse fell into disrepair. In 2005 the current owners, Broadland Properties, began a project to restore the old generating station and boathouse, which today are let as holiday accommodation.[21]

In the Lake District a row of crenellated boathouses is owned by the National Trust in the Fell Foot Country Park. They were built in 1869 for Colonel G. Ridehalgh of Fell Foot, who was one of the founder members of the Royal Windermere Yacht Club. The house no longer stands. The boathouses are built of local slate rubble, with slate roofs. They are modelled as miniature castles, with turrets, Gothic arches, embattled parapets, timber portcullis and arrow slits. They are used as a base for the Trust's boat-hire business at the southern end of Lake Windermere and as tea rooms.[22]

The Royal National Lifeboat Institution (RNLI) owns a great number of boathouses in Britain, mostly of utilitarian design. Many were built in the 1920s and often resemble rather dour-looking Methodist chapels. With larger boats now being used, the RNLI has an extensive building programme underway to construct new stations. 'In the past the RNLI employed engineers to design their lifeboat stations', but is 'now commissioning architects...for its more sensitive sites'. There has been a lifeboat station at Aldeburgh since the 1850s. The new Aldeburgh boathouse was designed by Mullins Dowse and Partners as an 'A' frame building; the 'A' frames are constructed of stainless steel, with a large door to accommodate the lifeboat. 'A free standing external gallery, like the bridge [of a ship], allows the public to look down into the boathouse when it is closed.'[23] The building also has an RNLI shop. The adjoining tractor shed mirrors the design of the boathouse.

British country estates are a rich source for boathouse design. The Crom Estate in County Fermanagh, Northern Ireland is owned by the National Trust, and is one of their most important nature conservation sites. A new castle was built on the estate in 1832-8 for the 3rd Earl of Erne, by the architect Edward Blore (1787-1879). Blore was well known for his country house practice and specialised in the Elizabethan and neo-Tudor styles.[24] Amongst other buildings on the estate is a splendid crenellated boathouse on the shores of its lake, echoing the design of the main house. The boathouse has a substantial upper story and impressive steps down to the water's edge.

Bowood in Wiltshire, the seat of the Marquis of Lansdowne, is another British estate with a significant boathouse. The Bowood boathouse sits rather grandly on the edge of a lake designed by the landscape architect 'Capability' Brown (1716-83). It is a traditional-looking timber-framed building, believed to date from the nineteenth century; built of brick and wood, with a slate roof and 'coronet' chimney, it is a perfect replica of a seventeenth-century English cottage. Only its veranda and steps to the water indicate its real purpose.

Kedleston Hall in Derbyshire was built in the 1760s by the first Baron Scarsdale to the design of Robert Adam (1728-92). The gardens have 'been restored in part' to an eighteenth-century 'pleasure ground' and it is within them that Robert Adam laid out his fishing pavilion, which sits in a series of lakes and cascades. It is without doubt the finest classical boathouse in Britain. The Fishing Room, as it is known, was built in 1771. The principal central section is pedimented, and has an imposing Venetian window, with a rusticated arch at water level. Both arch and pediment are replicated in the two boathouse wings, which sit to either side of the Fishing Room. In the chamber below the main room an underground spring bubbles into a stone basin in the floor, creating background water-music to the building. 'The main chamber of the Fishing Room, used for both fishing and dining, is decorated with four oil paintings of fish, a marble statue of Diana and various classical bas-reliefs'.[25]

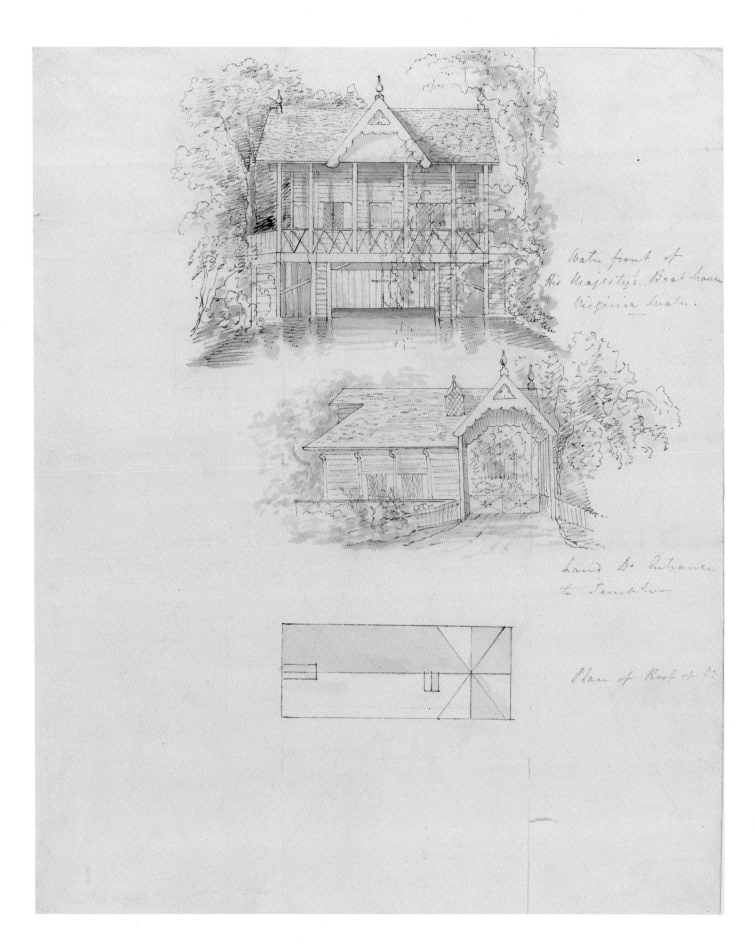

Water front of
His Majesty's Boat house
Virginia Water.

Land Do Entrance
to Temple

Plan of Roof of Do

The royal boathouses on Virginia Water, close to Windsor Castle, should also be included in this section on British boathouses. Although today only one boathouse survives, in the eighteenth century the lake was a haven for boating, housing an ornamental fleet and various buildings for royal entertainment. Their history is somewhat complex, but has been documented by Jane Roberts in her book *Royal Landscape - The Gardens and Parks of Windsor*.[26] Roberts illustrates Henry Flitcroft's design for the Boat house at Great Meadow Pond, c. 1748, noting that 'until the creation of Virginia Water a few years later', the Great Meadow Pond, 'was...the initial focus of the Duke of Cumberland's works in the Great Park'.[27] 'The first boat house was a small and elegant structure at the north-west corner of Great Meadow Pond, built in the late 1740s and shown on Vardy's 1750 plans'.[28] It is known that the 'original boathouse survived until the early nineteenth century.'[29] John Vardy (1718-65) was an English Palladian architect, who built Spencer House in London.[30] The Royal Collection holds a watercolour of another boathouse, dated 1829, by William Daniell. It shows 'The Boat-house [and] Fishing Temple' on the south bank of Virginia Water; the boathouse was later given an ornamental make-over to match the Fishing Temple, which was refashioned by the decorator Frederick Crace c. 1827.[31] In 1825, whilst building the new Boat-Man's House, Sir Jeffry Wyatville designed a new boathouse 'in a similar style to the Boat-Keeper's House'.[32] The Cooper-Hewitt Museum in New York holds a drawing of this design. Other boathouses were put up on Virginia Water, but these were of plainer design. By 1902 'the older boat houses were demolished' leaving 'the small brick boat house to the north of the island'.[33]

It would be a mistake to infer from these examples that the majority of British boathouses are rather grand, attached to large houses and architecturally superior. This is not so, the examples in this chapter merely illustrate the wide range of boathouse design in Britain. Our coastlines, lakes and rivers are well furnished with simple boathouses, of varying degrees of appeal, like most building types.

The distinction between British and worldwide boathouse design seems to come with our architectural history. The builders of British boathouses have enjoyed making miniatures of various architectural trends: the Gothic, Classic, neo-Tudor and the vernacular. Sometimes these are connected to the designs of grand houses, at other times they are purely the eccentric whim of a waterside dweller. Although fine examples are undoubtedly found on our country estates, the Thames provides an altogether more cosmopolitan environment: the rich and the not-so-rich living on its banks. Thames boathouses are therefore more representative of national fashions as a whole, and as such are probably more interesting to relate to boathouse form worldwide. So taking a journey down the Thames provides the best of opportunities to compare the grand, the simple, the old and the new in boathouse design.

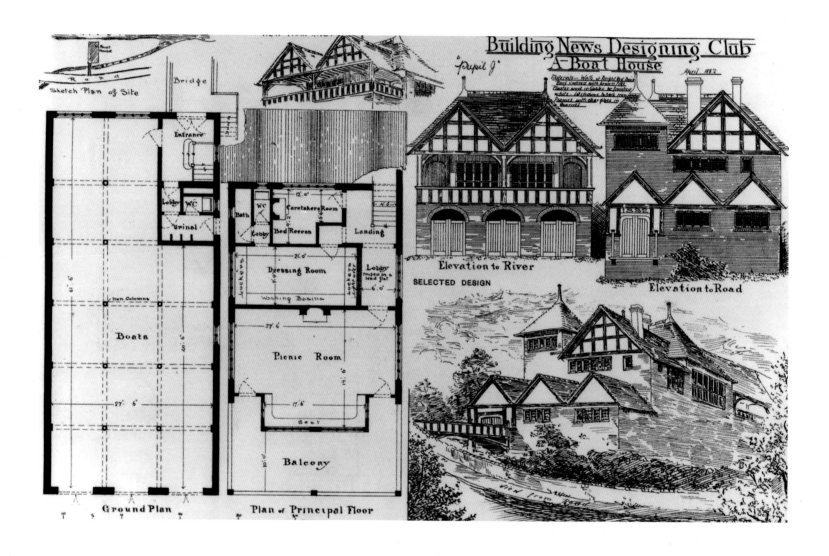

Chapter 3 : Thames Boathouses

A journey down the Thames shows a microcosm of boathouse design in much the same way as the worldwide view in Chapter 1. The non-tidal Thames is navigable from Lechlade, in Oxfordshire, down to Teddington in London where the tidal river continues on to the sea. It has over two hundred boathouses on its banks, some of which are exceptional in terms of their design or history. At Teddington the nature of the river changes dramatically; from here on it is the strength of the tidal force that determines the terrain – defences are stronger and boathouses have different conditions with which to contend. On the quieter upper stretches of the non-tidal river, governed by its locks, there is an extraordinary mixture of architectural styles: Swiss chalets, thatched idylls, castellated forts, eccentric Arts and Crafts, the opulent Edwardian Baroque and streamlined Art Deco. These mix easily with tin architecture and simple sheds on water. The grander examples sometimes reflect the architectural styling of their mother-house, in a similar way to the gatehouse of a large country estate.[34] Commercial and institutional examples, such as the buildings of boat-hire companies and rowing clubs, are generally less fanciful. Contemporary building has produced some exciting post-modern designs and three major boathouses have recently been built on the upper reaches of the Thames.[35]

Boathouses have existed in one form or another on the non-tidal Thames for centuries.[36] Early paintings and photographs show rural examples. By the late nineteenth century the private boathouse, built purely for leisure, created a notable change in river architecture. Increased leisure time, and legislation on the Thames in the late nineteenth century encouraged the boathouse building boom. A wider section of society was able, mainly as a result of employment legislation, to indulge in greater free time and relaxation. Many chose to spend their new found leisure time on the river. In 1866 the Thames Commissioners 'were empowered to administer the river';

later the Thames Preservation Act (1885) ensured that the Thames, above Teddington, was 'preserved for the purposes of public recreation;' this led to the building of the majority of boathouses that are illustrated.[37] The Thames, as an entity, is witness to constant change; boathouse building, from around the 1890s continues to be very much part of the developing picture of the built environment and of our society's changing leisure interests.

The early Thames boathouses tend to reflect the design of domestic housing of the period, sometimes at its most far-fetched. They connote status, wealth, or simply an interest. Built to house steam launches, varnished canoes, skiffs, motor and rowing boats, they provide private and independent leisure bases. Importantly too, through the private thoroughfare of the boathouse, they connect their owners to the countryside, nature and the aquatic life, providing an unrivalled sense of freedom into the river and its adventures beyond.

Boating people are often immersed in their aquatic life, demonstrating a mixture of romantic and practical in their natures. This unusual combination appears to have influenced nineteenth and early-twentieth-century boathouse building on the Thames. Later, this has included the somewhat brutalist twentieth-century boathouses with 'up-and-over garage doors', sometimes with concrete cladding, alongside a number of serious architectural statements, such as Terry Farrell's 1980s Henley Regatta Headquarters, and Shahriar Nasser's inspirational new boathouse for University College, Oxford. Amongst these contemporary designs is Balihoo, a private boathouse with living quarters, near Reading, which was the winner of the *Daily Telegraph* House of the Year, and an RIBA Downland prize in 1999.[38]

Bearing in mind the similarity of nineteenth-century Thames boathouses to the fashions of domestic housing, it seems that even the various ranges of terraced boathouses, which were generally built for commercial purposes, followed the same format. Distinctive features include a gabled roofline, balconied first-floor fenestration – this being the 'social floor' or level for human habitation – with the river level providing access for craft. Some have open entrances, whilst others sport barn-type doors. The base is generally constructed of brick, or a combination of brick and stone, with timbered or brick upper-sections. Many have decorative barge-boards and a wide variety of half-timbering in the neo-Tudor or mock Tudor style, or sculptural decoration making reference to Isis or Tamesis, as the Thames was often called.[39] Tiled roofs generally protect the boats from the elements and eyelets are often moulded into the roofline for ventilation. The commercially-produced nineteenth-century terracotta dragon is found grimacing menacingly on many a roofline. Some more fanciful domestic examples, where the boathouse is an integral part of the house, have turrets, oriel windows, balconies and platforms incorporated into their structure. Occasionally where the boathouse has upper floor accommodation there are two or sometimes three storeys. Others are simply barn-like sheds on water.

By the 1900s, in the heyday of boathouse-building, the building versus architecture debate was fuelled by the classicist Sir Reginald Blomfield (1856-1942), himself a boathouse architect. Blomfield championed the architect as artist, and promoted the 'grand manner' as seen in the classical architecture of Greece and Rome.[40] Also around this time the science of engineering entered the debate; interest in the subject was intense. *The Architectural Record* of 1891 contains an article on 'What is Architecture?' Whilst separating the 'science of construction' from the 'plan, masses and enrichment of structure...imagination of the artist...the art of building according to principles', the writer was keen to stress the qualities of beauty and harmony that were vital to the architecture of his period.[41] By the 1920s modernism had shifted architectural thinking to utility, form and function rather than decoration, whilst the importance of mass and plan had taken on a new meaning. Concepts of beauty and harmony change; the new University College Boathouse at Oxford with its glass and copper and under-decorated form, can be read as having qualities of harmony or beauty, but to compare these with the neo-classically decorated Edwardian Baroque or the rustic beauty of the Arts and Crafts is unproductive. Different ages seek widely ranging values in their aesthetics, materials and design.

A design competition should be an interesting exercise to realise the essential elements of a given genre. One such competition, for 'a Boating Clubhouse', a commercial venture, was published in the *Building News* of 1904. It looked for 'compactness and balance...in [the] plan, its river aspect being its most important feature, which should be 'dignified and befitting'; these seem rather vague terms today, but in the 1900s dignity in architecture was as important a component as eco-sustainability is today.[42] The competition conditions stipulated that this was a non-residential club, and that the building should have a billiard and reading-room, a kitchen, ladies' room with lavatory close by, dressing cubicles, two bathrooms, an office, a bicycle store, and a housekeeper's bedroom. It was to face the river and be built of brick and tile. Whilst this is a grandiose specification compared to that of the majority of private boathouses, it gives some idea of the requirements for institutional boathouse building of the period. If we look at the specification of an institutional boathouse today, such as the University College Boathouse or the Oxford University Boat Club (OUBC) it is not vastly dissimilar, bar gym and training facilities. The majority of private boathouses had, apart from boat accommodation, a far simpler layout of picnic or living room, a balcony, and at their most sophisticated, a bathroom and small kitchen.

Other domestic buildings of the period, stables and garages designed to house animals and machines, do not seem to have provoked such sentimentality, or even diversity. Stable blocks of large country houses were, as the architectural historian, Giles Worsley, has recounted, often grand classical affairs; but the motor car does not seem to have inspired such inventive design for its protection. With the rapid increase in the popularity of the car, the garage was also subject to design debate. Harrison-Townsend (1851-1928) architect of the Horniman Museum and Whitechapel Art Gallery in London gave a paper at the Architectural Association in 1908 on the subject of garage, or 'motor-house' design as it was known then. Size was of paramount importance: length, breadth and height, floor covering, ventilation, heating and the inspection pit; the latter involved a system of metal runners to guide the car onto the pit.[43] Some of these are not dissimilar to the basics required of a boathouse but, seemingly, the boathouse architects were allowed a more liberal and imaginative approach.

Nineteenth-century boathouses can sometimes seem to be architectural parodies, which can, at their most sentimental, veer towards a Wendy-house by the water. Nevertheless some serious architectural figures put their hand to boathouse design: the early-nineteenth-century classicist Robert Mylne's Temple of Neptune (1803) at Syon House for the Duke of Northumberland, the Victorian John Oldrid Scott's Oxford University Boathouse (1881) and Reginald Blomfield's late 1890s Wittington Boathouse at Medmenham are worthy examples of the genre.

It seems that some Thames boathouses represent a unique, if rather miniature part of our architectural history; they are aquatic swagger, built for show, on what is, after all, the Rotten Row of the boating world. The Thames is, as the historian Jonathan Schneer points out, an integral part of our nation's fabric, playing a role 'in some of the most notable events in British history': the Tudors used it as a road, a 'highway' for pageant, and for transporting their condemned to the Tower. The signing of the Magna Carta, arguably our most important constitutional document, took place at Runnymede, and its banks have witnessed the site of numerous battles, including that of the annual Oxford Cambridge Boat Race.[44] It is quite simply, Schneer claims 'England's river'.[45] The boathouses built on its banks are equally a part of England's history.

In total over two hundred and forty boathouses have been recorded between Lechlade and Teddington. This includes boathouses in some backwaters, where navigable.[46] Some have been converted for domestic or commercial purposes and only a selection have been singled out for their design, their history or simply their appeal. The sketch map of the Thames included on the endpapers shows the approximate location of the majority of the boathouses mentioned, for those who would like to follow a boathouse journey up or down the Thames.

Chapter 4 : The 1900s

The dawn of the age of the commuter saw pockets of rural land in the Thames valley being developed into enclaves for the middle classes and wealthy entrepreneurs who, whilst needing to be in daily reach of the capital, sought refuge and freedom in country and riverside-living. The geography of the Thames provided the perfect playground for leisure activities, whilst the area's railway network supported the travel requirements of its inhabitants. Susan Read, in her introduction to *The Thames of Henry Taunt* – the renowned Oxford photographer who published a guide to the Thames in 1872 – writes that 'the idea of "tourists" making excursions on the Thames appears to have become established from the beginning of the nineteenth century'. However it was 'during the 1880s [that] tourism on the Thames accelerated and flourished'.[47] The Thames Conservancy, who managed the river at the time, began formal licensing of pleasure craft during the 1880s. Wealthy river-dwellers such as Sir Frank Crisp at Henley and the Duke of Sutherland at Cliveden commissioned architects to design boathouses. Today swimming pools, gyms, tennis courts, jacuzzis and media-rooms are thought to lend similar prestige to a house. Despite the increasing thirst for speed the new vogue for 'athleticism' encouraged the use of the river, as a place for the exercise of muscle power and boating activity.

Shifts within the social and economic structure around the boom period of boathouse building on the Thames are revealing. Peter Bailey, writing on the subject of leisure in Victorian England, suggests that average 'wages rose gradually from the mid-century' with a 'remarkable expansion of the economy in the third quarter of the century'.[48] Changes to the legislative structure of the working week, such as a reduction in working hours in the mid 1860s, the Bank Holiday Act in 1871, which provided the basis of our national holidays, and the introduction of a Saturday half-holiday, collectively changed the work/leisure dynamic.[49] People literally had more time to themselves, and even more importantly for the building of boathouses, the rich and the super-rich had a sheer excess of time on their hands. The nineteenth-century social reformer Beatrice Webb (1858-1943) described how in 1900 'the rich are rolling in wealth and every class, except the sweated worker, has more than its accustomed livelihood'.[50] This section of society, labelled the 'new plutocracy,' whose livelihood was mainly based on trade and commerce, was expanding rapidly – the historian Thompson quotes a figure of 'some four million in 1901...[rising to] five million by 1911'.[51] New money generally searches for established status symbols, albeit with a 'new' edge. The middle classes viewed the life of the English country gentleman as the model for attainment; the need to emulate others seems an integral part of our human nature, we see it today in the way we ravenously consume the lives of the Beckhams, Kate Moss, film-stars such as George Clooney, and the lifestyles of new Russian oligarchs. Emulation of the upper classes in the nineteenth century led to an increase of small country house building; the Thames valley with its proximity to the capital was eminently suitable for such development. At Park Place, Henley in 1870 Thomas Cundy (1820-95) built a mansion for John Noble; the estate's picturesque boathouse on the Thames is earlier. Close by in the Hambleden valley the newly-knighted newsagent and bookseller W. H. Smith purchased the classical mansion

Greenlands,[52] The building is now the home of the Henley Management College. It still has its early rustic boathouse, which is believed to date from 1852, and was renovated in 1993. The 1876 Ordnance Survey map confirms its existence. Rather pleasingly the author of *Three Men in a Boat*, Jerome K. Jerome, refers to the sight of 'a quiet unassuming old gentleman [W.H. Smith himself] who may often be met with about these regions, during the summer months, sculling himself along in easy vigorous style' presumably from this very same boathouse.[53] At Medmenham, Hudson Kearley, the first Viscount Devonport and owner of International Stores, commissioned Reginald Blomfield to design a boathouse for his new estate. Further down the Thames, the grand and more opulent Cliveden (1851) built by Charles Barry for the second Duke of Sutherland, has a half-timbered boathouse in a parkland setting. This was designed by the vernacular-minded architect, George Devey (1820-86) c. 1857, who was 'an important precursor' to the Arts and Crafts movement.[54]

The historian Pearall writes that the countryside was seen as 'quaint and pretty'. Properties were cheap and the rapid expansion of the railways from the 1850s onwards – the branch railway line from Twyford to Henley was opened in 1857 – had brought easy and affordable accessibility for weekend retreats, whilst encouraging the city-dweller to buy into newly-built Edwardian enclaves in rural areas. Thames villages such as Goring and Shiplake still have many neo-Tudor houses dating from this period, varying from ten-bedroom mansions, to the more homely three-or four-bedroom country cottages. The greater part of the village of Medmenham on the Thames, between Henley and Marlow, was developed in the 1900s by the International Stores magnate, Hudson Kearley, as a prospective middle-class development. The architectural historian Mordaunt

Crook writes that at this time the 'shooting box and fishing lodge were now potential items in every plutocrat's portfolio'.[55] For those living on the banks of the Thames the boathouse was another essential that should be added to this list.

The super-rich were absorbed on their vast estates in the annual cycle of hunting, shooting and fishing. Reared on a diet of rugger, cricket and football from their public school days, their influence permeated into society, fostering a movement labelled the 'new athleticism', a nationwide interest in sport and the 'innovation of organised...athletic sports'.[56] Interest in sport generally, from the 1850s onwards, blossomed; historians of leisure seem to agree that the concept of 'modern leisure made its debut' around this time.[57] The choice was enormous: lawn-tennis, racing, bowling, football, boxing, tennis, croquet, golf, ice skating, walking, hockey, ping-pong – later known as table-tennis – pigeon and whippet racing and of course the major Edwardian passion, bicycling.[58] Peter Bailey describes how national bodies of sport, such as the Lawn Tennis and Boxing Federation were founded in this period, from the 1860s and 1870s onwards. Henley Rowing Club was founded in 1839 and Marlow Rowing Club in 1871.[59] John Leyland describes how 'The rise of Henley from an insignificant little meeting to the Royal Regatta of to-day is a notable illustration of the rapid development of public interest in athletics and out-door occupations during recent years'.[60] He describes how, by the late 1890s, 'there are thousands who delight in the enjoyment of the meeting and the social and river pleasures it brings'.[61] *The Pictorial Record*'s *Special Edition for Reading* described how 'every accommodation in the shape of boat-houses and boats is at hand [in the area]... in the summer the river is literally alive with crafts of all kinds'.[62]

But how people used their leisure-time was also a major social concern; alcohol consumption was at its height by the 1870s, and as an antidote 'abundant physical exercise,' endorsed by the self-help guru Samuel Smiles, was seen as a respectable and morally-improving alternative, to be pursued by the nation. The liberal politician and humanitarian C.F. Masterman, writing on *The Condition of England* in 1909 noted there was a general 'delight in fresh air [and in] the opportunities for 'sport' and exercise'.[63] It is therefore not difficult to see how a strong economic background, favourable legislation and a new-found interest in the countryside and open-air pursuits, led to a fascination in sport for all classes of society. Roy Hattersley's book, *The Edwardians*, confirms that in the countryside 'traditional 'sport' prospered as never before' citing shooting, racing, croquet, tennis, football, cricket, boxing, tennis and hiking. 'The whole country', he wrote' found time for pleasure', sport became 'the true opiate of the English masses.'[64] Access to the river was free, so participation in water activities was egalitarian. Late-nineteenth-century pictures of the locks during the summer months often show a river almost full to bursting point, with boats and people and onlookers, seemingly from every walk of life.[65] Both photography and print record the boathouse phenomenon. This national absorption with sport and leisure manifested itself on the Thames by an increase in boating and boathouse building.

5.1 A Rustic Boathouse on the Upper Reaches
John Clarke 2005

Chapter 5 : Lechdale to Oxford

Taking a boat from Lechlade to Oxford on a sunny day is a magical experience. But to the boathouse-hunter, this stretch of hairpin-meandering river, through flat green pastures full of contented cattle, seems worryingly bereft of boathouses.[66] The writer Hilaire Belloc describes the Thames as the 'highway of Southern England', a 'permanent means of travel' an 'obstacle, a defence, and a boundary,' statements which still seem relevant today, a hundred years on.[67] The most noticeable buildings on this least-developed part of the Thames, apart from the lock-keepers' cottages, are the squat concrete pillboxes, built as a line of machine-gun emplacements to guard against the invader during World War II. Footbridges, reed beds, and the low-arched stone bridges, built of great hewn blocks, are some of the few features, in what is essentially an almost primeval landscape.

The river flows past Kelmscott, the 'manor [of William] Morris,' which Belloc describes 'with its garden close to the river, a boathouse and all things handy'.[68] Quoting a letter from William Morris, the historian Jonathan Schneer, writes that 'perhaps best of all he [William Morris] loved that the 'baby Thames' 'was near by, just a hundred yards down a dirt track to the little wooden pier and boathouse'.[69] Neither the boathouse nor the pier any longer exist, but their mental footprint gives a pleasing start to the search for Thames boathouses. This part of rural England was paradise for Morris; its present was deeply etched by its past, paying little respect to the industrial future, which so disturbed Morris and his followers.

Closer to Northmoor Lock are two rustic boathouses, of which Morris would have approved - one with a weathervane and open gates, the second evocatively named 'Eden's End,' in a more dilapidated state. A third wet boathouse on this reach stands on the site of an earlier boathouse, and is owned by the Blackwell family. It is simply but elegantly built of cedar, with a triangular glass insert at its river gable. The Blackwells made expeditions from the early boathouse in their skiff, and still follow that tradition. The boathouse was built by White's of Appleton in the same style and shape as the original. The owner and chef at the local inn at Fyfield, two miles from Appleton, catches crayfish for his restaurant in the boathouse field. This appears on the menu, rather poetically described, as 'crayfish caught from Toby's field'.

A little further downstream is a substantial modern house, with a large integral round-arched dock; this is the largest boathouse on the reach, and is designed in a contemporary neo-Tudor style. It looks to the past, with gables, leaded windows, hanging tiles and balconies, using brick, wood, stone and wrought-iron work.

Chapter 6 : Oxford to Reading

The rural back land of the upper reaches changes, as the city of Oxford approaches; small sections of boat industry, allotments, and newly-renovated back-to-back housing border the river. The landscape slowly, but noticeably smartens up. At Oxford, the scene changes dramatically into a river busy with motor boats, punts and rowers. Folly Bridge marks the start of this. In the late nineteenth century Salter's boathouse and barge were located on the site of the Head of the River pub, by the bridge; their business as 'boat-builders and steam operators' dates back to 1858. Their base and slipway is now on the opposite side. Salter's premises were reputedly burnt down by the Suffragettes in 1913, but were re-built shortly after.[70] About a decade earlier John Leyland wrote: 'It may be said...that Oxford University men discovered the river – discovered, that is, the river in a boating sense.'[71] A few hundred yards down river we can see the legacy of his statement.

The collection of ten college boathouses on Christ Church Meadows at Oxford, below Folly Bridge, is the first sight of real boathouse building on our journey. Their presence shows the utilitarian demands of the University, from the 1930s onwards, when the college barges, with their high maintenance costs and limited space, which were used as club houses for the rowing, had ceased to serve their purpose. In their place came the functionalism of the post-war boathouse in paired arrangements: russet red brick and wood cladding with generous boathouse bays, flat roofs, large balconies, flag poles and college insignia. The first boathouses in this group were described, in 1956, by the architect Diana Rowntree, in an attack on modernism, as 'brick cube[s]' and 'grimly' functional.[72] One or two later ones make attempts at the Art Deco, with spiral outer staircases and more rounded lines, but generally, as a group, they make for an unprepossessing architectural statement. Some are individual college boathouses, others have shared possession. Judith Curthoys, the Christ Church archivist, writes that 'there was a proposal to replace the Christ Church barge with a boathouse as early as 1907' but that their boathouse, the first, was eventually built in 1935, followed by the Magdalen, Trinity, Merton, and Worcester boathouses in 1939. By 1956 seven more were at the design stage.[73] Rowntree praised the architectural 'immediacy' of the barges; she found the new boathouses alienating, and called for boathouse architects to seek 'integration' with their water and surroundings.

One of the more notable institutional boathouses built on the Thames was the Oxford University Boathouse, which was east of Folly Bridge, on the opposite bank to the college boathouses. Built in 1880-1 to the designs of John Oldrid Scott (1841-1913) as the centre for Oxford rowing, it was an imposing almost pyramidal affair, with wide ground floor bays for boat storage, protected by four shallow arched double doors. The first-floor balustered balcony provided a panoramic viewing area over the river; the tall half-timbered three-bay central gable, with cross-wings and rising Tudor chimneys, contained an assortment of rooms for recreational purposes. After burning down accidentally during the building process in 1881, the building sadly suffered its final indignity, by fire, in September 1999.[74] When the OUBC, the Oxford University Boat Club, took over the premises as their headquarters in 1881 it may well have been regarded as a prototype for nineteenth-century boathouse building on the Thames. Contemporary records have it down as 'a rather ugly affair', although the Oxford photographer Henry Taunt heroically described it as 'picturesque'.[75]

The University College archives hold a collection of letters concerning the building and design of the OUBC boathouse, which show that the design process was far from easy. The college 'rented out land [which was part of Eastwick Farm] for the building of a boathouse for the OUBC'. A letter dated 24th March 1880 from the architect John Oldrid Scott to Charles Faulkner (1833-1892) the Bursar of the College, states 'I have seen Mr Courtney [the OUBC Treasurer and Bursar to New College] and I am glad to find that he fully approves of my declining at this stage to make an alteration in my design'.[76] A pencil note on the letter from Faulkner states 'This is all flummery. I saw Courtney at Oxford on the morning of the 25th and he said that he didn't care a button one way or the other....and was only anxious to get the thing done somehow'. Oldrid Scott continued, somewhat unctuously, in his letter

'You will feel that I am acting in the only way open to an architect who really cares for his art'.

Continuing correspondence from Faulkner to the University College Fellow E. J. Payne (1872-1904) on the subject states 'The cool way in which he [Scott] "declines" to make any alteration is only a preliminary to agreeing to anything you insist upon...What we insist on is less obtrusiveness in form, and if possible in colour...Take a pen and red ink and ruthlessly cut his elevation down...The River has hitherto been secure from these monstrosities...Judging Bodley... [the architect who designed the Master's Lodgings at University College] I don't think his taste is much better than Scott's'.[77]A further letter from Courtney to Faulkner indicates that 'Rowe consents to join me in putting pressure on Scott to alter the chimneys'.[78] These were tall with inset brick arches, a feature which Scott defended as important to the design. The chimneys were finally subject to a 'slight alteration,' but remained a striking feature of the building. In the Bursar's Notes of June 24th 1880, Faulkner writes: 'Payne and I were desired to 'use our best endeavours' to get some alteration in the hideous design of the building proposed by J. Oldrid Scott. We did so; but with very small result'.[79] The building itself was successfully used for over a hundred years as a boathouse, whether the design was appreciated or not. Its generous balcony area was always heaving during the Torpids and Bumps race weeks.

6.3 University College Boathouse, Oxford
With kind permission of the Master and Fellows of University College, Oxford
Belsize Architects Nick Kane 2006

After a fire in 1999 totally destroyed the OUBC building, an enlightened group of University College fellows obtained planning consent for a new clubhouse for the College on the site, having selected the design of Shahriar Nasser of Belsize Architects from a group of chosen competing architects. The design was to be sympathetic to the surroundings and the life of the old building, show a sense of care for conservation and biodiversity, whilst addressing the needs of present day collegiate rowing. The result is exciting. Blue-toned brick to the ground floor, with four boat bays at river level, and a glazed off-centre entrance, create a low-lying horizontal boat storage space.[80] To the first floor a central cantilevered glass viewing box – the clubhouse area – gives drama to the composition, which is balanced by open balconies, protected by the eaves of copper-clad roofing, the shape of which is intended to signify a 'hovering blade'. Facilities include a boat repair bay, changing rooms and showers, a club room, with accommodation for students and a caretaker, echoing those of the old boathouse. The elevation of the accommodation is clad in horizontal cedar slats, which protect the walls, and also act as shutters over the windows on the first floor. Provision has been made for adequate security in an area which can feel unprotected at night. This is an inspired design which makes use of geometrical shapes, the square and the rectangle, yet despite of this retains a sense of fluidity in deference to its river setting. The building was opened by Lord Moynihan, Chairman of the British Olympic Association in May 2006, and was built by the Kidlington firm of Kingerlee. The building received an RIBA South Award in June 2008.

6.4 University College Boathouse, Oxford (by day and night)

With kind permission of the Master and Fellows of University College, Oxford

Belsize Architects Nick Kane 2006

overleaf: **6.5 The Clubroom, University College Boathouse, Oxford**

With kind permission of the Master and Fellows of University College, Oxford

Belsize Architects Nick Kane 2006

Further down river stands Long Bridges Boathouse belonging to Hertford College, used also by Mansfield, St Catharine's, St Hilda's, Templeton Green and City Barge. The three utilitarian brick bays of the earlier building were re-modelled in 1996 to create a new building with five distinctive first-floor blue bays, a balcony and flagpoles corresponding to the timbered gables. The boat bays sit below. Richard Norton, an old Hertford member, writes that there have been three previous occupants of the site: the famous boat builder John Clasper and later the firms of F. Roughs and then Tims, whose names will be familiar to river historians. Henry Taunt describes the Long Bridges, a quarter of a mile down from the OUBC, 'with F. Rough's Boat House just above.'[81] The earlier boathouse on the site was burnt down by Suffragettes in 1915.

Just before Donnington Bridge, there is the opportunity to glance back to the past. The second Corpus Christi barge (1930) nestles secretively in a backwater of pollarded willows, giving a nostalgic flashback to the first clubhouses for Oxford rowing. Donnington Bridge graffiti wakes the passer-by up to real life. Immediately after Donnington Bridge is the 1970s Oxford Rowing Club boathouse with two blue boat bays to the ground floor. Stocky rectangles, using brick and concrete with two broad boathouse bays, a large balcony, picture windows, and an outer staircase are embellished with a gesture of wood cladding. Function and economics inevitably outplay any attempt at aesthetics. It serves its purpose and is not unpalatable. The industrial wing of Salter Brothers is close by; it is a large two shed structure with corrugated iron roofs, and two vast sliding doors accessed by sheet piled channels.

The Isis Boathouse stands just before Iffley Lock, an unprepossessing two-bay red brick building with two first floor windows, and half-timbered gable, providing storage for skiffs and sculls – rowing boats – alike. This is believed to have been built in 1905 by the Beesley family, with the Isis Cottage, which sits next door to the boathouse, a few years later. In the 1930s it was sold to the famous boat builder, George Harris, who used it for the building of eights; his son David took over the building and business and built the annex attached to the boathouse. Today the boathouse is privately owned and has been converted to include accommodation. A wooden balcony and flagpole has considerably improved its appearance, and plans are underway to renovate the internal space, keeping its traditional boat-storage space below. In the past Oxford Brookes and previously Oxford Polytechnic, used the building for land training; it is currently used by a new club, the 'Oxford Academicals'. The Isis Boathouse is a lucky survivor of utilitarian building practices, which is happily reaping the benefits of a sensitive restoration.

At Iffley Lock the lock-keeper's house stands guard. On the opposite bank is a skiff-roller under a stone bridge, providing a ground-based passage for the punt and skiff fraternity to bypass the lock. After the lock, the river enters a green jungle world of willows and lone fishermen. Two miles on from Sandford Lock, the deepest lock on the Thames, is Radley College boathouse, a rowing complex of two boathouses: the first a white breeze-block four-bay building dated 1922, the second a red brick, four-bay building with a balcony. The complex has a slipway, pontoons and a wooden bridge. A caretaker's cottage has been built by its side.

The Reverend V. Hope's Appendix on Rowing in *The History of Radley College* 1847-1947 describes 'that even before the College was actually founded, the first Warden, R. C. Singleton, realized the need for boating facilities. In recording a walk which he took down by the river on June 4th 1847, he remarked in his diary 'We were not struck by any suitable place in the neighbourhood of Radley for a boathouse'. A boathouse was however found by 1849, a little above the Nuneham Boathouse.[82] Rowing continued from this building until 1854; later a small floating boathouse was used near the lock and in 1861 a wooden boathouse was built for the college on the bank at Sandford. This was replaced in 1889 and stayed in use until 1921. In 1911 the Evans Boathouse was built opposite the island, in memory of an old Radley coach.

A pupil of 1923, Phillip Gurdon, reminisced many years later of the rowing at that time:

'One morning Messrs Savory and Howard chose 6 boys and me as cox, took us to Sandford where an eight was lying - I don't know where she came from. We all got in and rowed her to the new boat-house...In those days there were no straw hats, or flannels: we had to play in our ordinary clothes. To row in cloth trowsers [sic] white shirts with starched fronts and collars attached and college caps [that is, mortar-boards] on yr [sic] head is not an exhilarating pastime, and there was no rush for it.'[83]

The 1922 boathouse, the oldest on the present site, is one that is perhaps unusual in school culture of today. In the Easter holidays of 1921 'gangs of boys, masters and Old Radleians, working under two foremen, began the work, digging the foundations, raising the floor level, and unloading gravel from barges.' They completed the walls by the Summer Term and the boathouse, though not finished, was used for their summer races that year. 'Subsequent additions have been the cut (largely dug by boy [sic] labour in April, 1922)...the boatman's bungalow in 1928 and the small swimming pool for teaching the 'unpassed' in 1929.' In 1966 the new Howard Boathouse was built by the architect, Peter Sutherland, of Henley, to the right of the old one, providing more boat storage, a first-floor clubroom, showers and the Boatman's flat. The boathouse has to be interpreted as a great lesson in group activity; it still stands and is in use today.

6.7 The Boathouse at Lower Radley with the Boatman's Cottage c. 1930

Radley College

The boat-house at Nuneham c. 1907 is the first important
example of the neo-Tudor on our journey down the Thames; it is
a picturesque sight on this stretch of the river.[84] Its bulk is
pebble-dashed, showing buttresses in the Arts and Crafts
tradition, with a decorated gable, whose elaborate black and
white timber-work is cut in a circular pattern. The full width
fenestration is protected by a wooden balcony, supported by
giant brackets. The gable is framed by a decorative barge-board.
A singular oriel window sits to a side elevation. Arts and Crafts
influence is seen in the scrolled ironwork and the heart motifs
cut in the balusters. The building has real 'gingerbread' appeal.
Taunt describes how Nuneham was the seat of the Harcourt
family, set in a 1,200 acre park and a favourite place for 'water
parties from Oxford'; its gardens, with a rock grotto, were
renowned. The boathouse would probably have been integral to
this scheme.

An article in *The Building News* of April 1907 reports that the
new boat-house 'is now in course of erection in the park at
Nuneham on [the] site of [the] old boat-house…[for] the Right.
Hon. L. Harcourt M.P.' Stephen Salter FRIBA, of the Oxford
Salter's boat building family was the architect.[85] 'The building
gives accommodation for a launch, two punts, gigs etc…with end
and side gangway in boathouse, and pulleys for slinging boats to
roof. There will be a large balcony towards the river, where there
is a large tea-room, besides kitchen and offices…The walls are
[36cm] thick, built of cement concrete and rough-cast. The roof
is covered with green tiles, made specially for the job. The site is
a very beautiful one, embowered in trees, and with sloping
woodlands and hills at rear.' This is a rare description of a
boathouse in a trade magazine of the period, and is useful for an
insight into the level of facilities such a building would be
expected to provide.

6.10 Abingdon School Boathouse
Abingdon School 2005

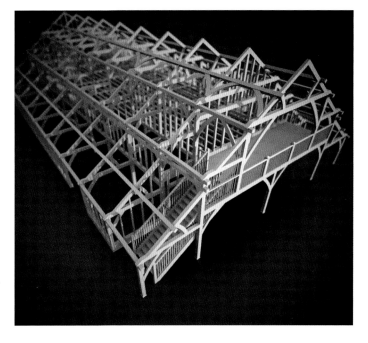

At Abingdon Lock, where gunnera plants stand like giant umbrellas, life seem to stand still on the river; however the church spire beckons and there is a sense of civilization on the horizon. In 1907 Hilaire Belloc reminded his readers of the great monasteries and priories which were to be found all along the Thames; the abbey of Osney, the Cluniac abbey at Reading and the Benedictine abbeys of Abingdon, Chertsey and Westminster, along 'with a string of dependent houses and small foundations which line[ed] the river'. These 'great monastic houses founded a tradition of local wealth which has profoundly affected the history of the Thames valley', which Belloc described, even then as 'the economic power of England'.[86] The great chimneys of the almshouses, the imposing stone bridge and the site of the original junction of the Wiltshire and Berkshire canal suggest a notable meeting point. Henry Taunt records that the boat builder and hirer, J. Stevens, had premises at Abingdon in the nineteenth century, just above the bridge. The 1932 Ordnance Survey map shows a boathouse at Abingdon on the island just after the bridge.

A little further on is Abingdon School's 'A' framed timber boathouse, with simple circular-edged bargeboards, and a full-width balcony, protected by a sweeping tiled roof. The ground-floor boat-bays have sliding timber doors. This is an essay in timber, internally resembling a sixteenth-century aisled barn, with a hint of the Swiss chalet aesthetic. It is in fact a modern hybrid of traditional timber-framing. Like many institutional boathouses, the motivation to build came from a winning boat. The parents of the School's First VIII of 2002, spurred on by having won a triumvirate of races, including The Princess Elizabeth Challenge Cup at Henley 'led a parent-school partnership to build a new boathouse'.[87] This was spearheaded by Norman Guiver, whose son was in the boat. They achieved something quite remarkable, a building which some have

claimed to rank among the 'largest [contemporary] oak framed buildings [to be] erected in the UK' standing at 30m x 17.5m x 8.5m. '70 timber-framers from around the world [from America, Canada, France, Holland, Ireland and Wales] turned up...to cut the first 4 frames of 10 and raise them on site [like the great Amish gatherings] with a gin pole in just ten days'.[88] The frame was cut on the rugby pitch and transported to the site. The front half of the building, including the balcony and two bays took nine days to erect, the back half being completed by the Timber Frame Company of Somerset. It was a group effort of gigantic proportions; the two hundred and sixty-three people involved created a spirit which will remain forever with the building and the Boat Club. It has fostered tremendous pride within the school; the upper half of the building is fitted out with a gym, which is also used by parents. The building was opened by the Olympic oarsman Sir Matthew Pinsent in October 2003.

6.12 The Clifton Hampden Thatched Boathouses
John Clarke 2005

Abingdon School's timbered masterpiece reflects the rural nature of this stretch of the Thames. Undergrowth worthy of a journey on Bogart's *African Queen* follows the route to Culham Lock.[89] This is bridge, not boathouse territory: first comes Sutton's stone footbridge, with a low clearance, the Appleford railway bridge follows soon after, and then Clifton Lock, followed by Clifton Hampden's red brick Gothic, designed by Sir George Gilbert Scott (1811-78), famous for his St Pancras Station Hotel in London (1868), the Albert Memorial (1861) and the Foreign Office (1856). Cattle wallow like buffalo and crested grebe dabble on this stretch of the Thames, which is bereft of boathouse building. Interestingly the 1932 Ordnance Survey map shows 'boathouses' at Appleford on this reach, and records six boathouses at Long Wittenham, none of which exist now. Such is the sleepiness today of this part of the river that one river lounger has hoisted a vast armchair on the top of his narrow boat, to provide a platform, on which to while away his time.

The bend in the river at Clifton Hampden brings our first pair of boathouses into view. They are thatched with a diamond-patterned stick work set into the gable, with timber side elevations and loosely-slatted central gates, providing access for the boats. They are believed to have been built c. 1900, and have been in the same family for five generations.

Further on, opposite Clifton Meadows, there is a more substantial brick boathouse, in the grounds of what was a large 1900s house, now converted into flats. This has a timbered gable with circular braces, and a grand balcony with panoramic views. Its long roofline is distinctive, with a crocketed terracotta finial and cupola. It is a dry boathouse with water access below. Things are looking up.

The bend in the river at Shillingford reveals a pleasantly dilapidated barn-type boathouse, with its thatch slipping away, and its slatted water-gates just holding their own. It stands in front of a substantial brick and flint house, with river frontage. The boathouse is believed to date from the nineteenth century, and is still in regular use. A family event is held roughly every five years to dredge out the acrid mud.

Directly opposite stands a truly substantial neo-Tudor boathouse, with a Tudor-arched opening to the base of its brick and flint construction. Such a proud and lofty construction could be found on the high street of many an English town. It shows a first-floor balcony before a treble-arched range on the first floor, and a small central window set into the apex of the hipped roof. The building dates from the 1890s, and represents vernacular boathouse building at its most extravagant. Folklore recounts that Shillingford Court, to which the boathouse originally belonged, was built by Frederick Martin, the tailor to the Prince of Wales, and that it was here, reputedly, that Lillie Langtry and other acquaintances of the future Edward VII, were entertained. It very grandly housed a ballroom on the first floor, with its original oak floor still in place. There was also a minstrel's gallery served by two spiral staircases, where presumably the band played for dancing. The staircases are still intact but have been moved, so that the gallery could be extended. The balcony overlooking the river was originally open, but has now been glazed. The property is reputed to have been one of the first in the area to have a telephone installed, perhaps as a necessity for one of its more demanding occupants.

A little further on a wildly-overgrown boathouse comes into view, clad in clap-board with a terracotta tiled roof; it appears to be completely abandoned, its gates stand open, tantalisingly revealing a boat within. Other boathouses follow before Day's Lock; they are of little architectural pretension, but serve their purpose. Next on this reach is a rather jaunty boathouse on a pebble-dashed base with an outer wooden staircase, a strong balcony supported by 'Y' framed timbers, and timber-clad upper elevations. The building was originally built completely of timber, but the lower section was replaced in the 1980s with block-work. This boathouse has been one family's haven since the 1900s.

The Ferry House at Shillingford, just before Shillingford Bridge, shows its choice of the neo-Tudor as the perfect dressing for the smart nineteenth-century boathouse. Its singular gable was decorated with barge-boards, and is supported by ogee half-timbering to the balcony elevation. The elongated chimney shows the domestic nature of this boathouse. The latrine hut was set away to the side of the building. John Loudon's nineteenth-century design compendium for cottage, farm and villa architecture features a 'Cottage Dwelling in the German Swiss style', which shows many similar design features to the Shillingford Bridge boathouse: brick or stone foundations with a first storey, exterior staircase, wooden first floor, and a balcony.[90] Interestingly, Loudon suggests that 'Were such a building to be erected in England, it could only be for the sake of its character....therefore the proper situation for it would be in a romantic woody vale, glen or dingle...where the appearance of such a cottage would raise up interesting associations in the mind of the continental traveller'.[91] The German architectural historian, Nicholas Pevsner, describes this area as 'a pretty stretch of the Thames, with willow trees', which supports the idea of a picturesque setting for such a building.[92]

The boathouse is believed to have been built between 1898 and 1902 and belonged to Ferry House, which stands close to the bridge.[93] The distinctive dappled brickwork, set in geometric patterns, makes it unusual. The bricks used were in fact broken ones, retrieved from the bottom of the kiln, giving the building a painterly edge, rather like a piece of Kaffe Fassett knitwear. In the last century Ferry House and the boathouse were owned by the family who made Gainsborough chocolates for Woolworths. The house, estate, two Rolls Royces and the boathouse were left to their gardener, who eventually sold them on. The present owners are planning to restore the building to its original wet boathouse status. The early photograph shows the boathouse in a manicured setting with a trim garden and pergola-walk.

6.16 The Boat House, Howbery Park c. 1906

The David Beasley Collection c. 1906

THE BOAT HOUSE HOWBERY PARK

After Benson Lock the most individual Arts and Crafts
boathouse that the Thames could possibly produce, stands high
like a fairy-tale structure for all to see.[94] This belonged to the
estate of Howbery Park, and was built on the site of an earlier
boathouse, by the American Mr Harvey Du Cros, the Dunlop
millionaire, in 1906, by Wheelers of Reading.[95] Howbery Park
was requisitioned in the Second World War; afterwards the site
became derelict. It was later sold by Lord and Lady Wittenham,
and developed into a business park. In 1949 the boathouse
became the responsibility of the firm HR Wallingford, a water
research company; their employees have used it ever since. It is
a great credit to the company that the building still exists.
Originally the boathouse had three staircases, one on the side,
one to the rear and the spiral at the front, but two of these have
since been dismantled. The highly picturesque photograph of
1906 shows two of these staircases, with fretwork balustrade
and a diamond-patterned balcony. Apparently Lady Wittenham
often took tea in her boathouse, summoning her servants with a
bell, which was connected to the main house.

6.18 The Wallingford neo-Baroque Boathouse

The RIBA Photographs Collection *The Architect* 1882

6.19 The Wallingford neo-Baroque Boathouse

Robert James Photography 2007

Today the boathouse looks less ornate, but still deserves the care it has been given. With distinctive sweeping slatted gates its brick sides support a half-timbered cottage which stands high above water level, with Tudor chimney, a red door and a gaily painted green-blue balcony. Its neo-Tudor timbering is painted in the same colour. Adjoining and to its side, is the wooden spiral staircase, whose balusters sweep up to the balcony, supported by elongated verticals which carry on upwards to a tiled conical roof. The effect is vernacular, artistic and inspiring.

Wallingford follows; an early photograph shows the commercial boathouses on the town's banks, with their boats for hire. *Salter's Guide to the Thames* marks this as Corneby's boathouse. Its three-bay neo-Tudor gables and balconies set the recreational scene for the more serious work below. Today a pub, appropriately named 'The Boathouse' makes easy use of the site and buildings. Turner's boathouse was just after St Leonard's church. The 1910 Ordnance Survey Map shows a boathouse at Winterbrook, downstream of Wallingford, and another at Mongewell Park on this stretch.

The simplicity of Wallingford Rowing Club's brick and tile structure stands in contrast to its neighbour, the neo-Baroque boathouse, a more serious and learned example of boathouse architecture. Using the language of the Baroque the architect plays with a Diocletian window to water level - this semicircular window was found in the Roman baths of Diocletian A.D. 306. The boathouse also has a generously columned veranda, a large pedimented bay window and a ball-topped cupola decorates the roofline. It is impeccably maintained, and is probably the most important example of the Edwardian Baroque on the non-tidal Thames.[96] It formerly belonged to a large house called Riverside, and was built to the designs of Messrs Christopher and White in 1882, for the artist G.D. Leslie RA.[97] Its design was featured in *The Architect* of that year. It is described as being built 'solidly of local red bricks; the upper portion of the walls are plastered, the exposed woodwork is of oak, and the roof is finished with Coalbrookdale plain tiles and lead'. The builder was J. Weller of Wallingford. Leslie dated its building as 1887. He also describes a boathouse close by, occupied by an artist friend, Mr Hayllar, as being 'very quaint, running askew from the river beneath the shade of the elms, over it is an old-fashioned bow-windowed summer house'.[98] This is definitely the first, and perhaps the only mention of a boat house with a bow window.

6.20 The OUBC Fleming Boathouse, Wallingford

Oxford University Boat Club Tuke Manton Architects

Philip Searle 2007

overleaf: **6.21 The Boathouse, OUBC, Wallingford**
Oxford University Boat Club Tuke Manton Architects
Big Blade Photography 2007

The internal shot of the boathouse shows the stacked eights. This part of the
building is designed so that in the event of the river flooding water flows through.
This was successfully tested in the floods of 2007.

This stretch of the Thames seems to generate big ideas for boathouse building. The OUBC – Oxford University Boat Club – have just finished building a mega-complex at Wallingford, with both wet and dry boathouses as a base for their rowing activities. Built of reinforced concrete and a steel frame, clad in brickwork, the building has a maintenance-free Terne-coated stainless steel roof, with secret gutters. Other materials, such as the appropriately named Eternit Lamina External, are used for soffits and fascias. Design features include brick plinths in Blue Staffords to the base of the building, spiral staircases, two large but varied gables, inset with dark blue powder-coated fascias and glass inserts. The deep wrap-round balcony stretches the full river elevation of the complex. Even the door heights, set at 2.1 metres are unusual, catering for the average size of the occupants of this boathouse for giants. Tuke Manton Architects – Peter Tuke was a Blue in 1966 – with guiding input from Steve Royle, the Director of Rowing at Oxford, have created a boathouse and training facility on a par with a top racehorse stud. It has the aesthetic of an office complex, and is a machine to produce machines. The dry boathouse area has three vast bays, with an extensive drive-through maintenance bay. The mechanical and electrical equipment, housed in a plant room, would grace any trans-Atlantic liner. The size and proportions are imperial, not in a mathematical sense, but in order to achieve an easy working space for the purpose. The end result is that the scale and size reflect the might and grandeur of the institution. The river elevation of the dry boathouse has three Diocletian windows and internal grilled water-gates to allow flood flow through this level, should the river rise, as it sometimes does in this area. These are also found to the side of the wet boathouse, which houses the coaching launches and

Bosporos, the Oxford boat race launch. The use of the Diocletian window in this context connects the building historically to architecture and to water. The middle curved section of the building houses the human element of this power-house: briefing, ergo and treatment rooms, utilities, drying-rooms, male and female showers, kitchen and offices. There are two clubrooms: the central one over the dry boathouse has a gallery, which will be used to display the club's memorabilia. The second clubroom is over the wet boathouse; this will be used for dining and other functions, having a capacity for 50 plus people. Adjoining this is the boathouse manager's flat. Using traditional gables the architect has created a low-based plan, defended from the river by brick plinths, with pontoons and attractive bridging that allows the Thames path to pass in front of the building. The boathouse contains all the amenities necessary for state-of-the-art twenty-first century rowing. The letters OUBC, painted in dark blue, are massively wrought in galvanised steel on the water-gates of the dock. The blue OUBC flag flies at the heart of the complex. The building has been funded by the generosity of the Old Blues; it was opened by Robin Fleming on 10th June 2007, in memory of his father, Philip Fleming, who rowed in the 1910 Blue Boat. It is to be known officially as the OUBC Fleming Boat House. The building suggests that the power and ego of the OUBC is rock-solid for future generations.

6.22 Agatha Christie's Clap-board Boathouse

John Clarke 2005

6.23 Carmel College Boathouse
John Clarke 2005

Soon after, in complete contrast to the high technology of the OUBC, stands the quintessential clap-board boathouse, once owned by Agatha Christie. It is a simple gable in beach hut mode, with a hint of barge-boards, and a corrugated iron roof – what could be finer – its beauty is defined by its simple use of material and rustic charm.

The Carmel College Boathouse certainly can claim architectural pretension, but is in need of restoration. The boarding school of Carmel College no longer exists; Comer Homes, who now own the site, are currently seeking planning permission for adult educational buildings and a retirement village. The boathouse, together with the ruined church of St John The Baptist, alongside the river are hauntingly special. The boathouse elevation facing Mongewell House is a particularly fine example of the neo-Tudor, with shaped timbers, patterned brickwork, a tiled gable and glazed windows. The gatehouse to the estate has a date-plaque of 1889, with the initials ACF. *Salter's Guide to the Thames* notes that 'the present red brick mansion [was] erected by Mr. A.C. Fraser' in 1889.[99] The original house is believed to have been built for the Bishop of Durham. The principal boathouse section is of brick and clay-tiled construction, with a large gable housing the projecting boat bay entrance, guarded by a stocky, square-framed portcullis gate. To its side stands a dry boathouse with a flat roof, and a balustraded viewing platform. Its mellow brick construction, with brick buttresses, and a mullioned stone window are in the Arts and Crafts vernacular; surprisingly inside is a disused armaments depot, another relic of World War II defences. This gem of a boathouse will hopefully soon be restored, and put back to use. [100]

6.24 The Cariad Boathouse and Howgate Boathouse
The Museum of Rural Life University of Reading c. 1900s

Carriad, Goring   C464

There follows an assortment of rowing club – Oxford Brookes – and clap-board boathouses, both new and old, which are brightly interspersed with the tin-shed architecture of Sheridan Marine, offering fuel and chandlery to the river. There is a 1950s Isle of Wight feel to this little haven, which shows that a commercial structure can offer a cheery, yet utilitarian alternative. We are now on a gastronomic stretch of the river where the old wooden boathouse, at the Beetle and Wedge Hotel, has been transformed into a restaurant. Further down is the Old Leatherne Bottel Inn, which Leyland shows as having a simple rustic boathouse in the 1890s, but which today no longer exists.

In complete contrast close to Cleeve Lock, in a backwater, stood a rustic boathouse at Cleeve Mill; the mill itself is believed to have been built in the late sixteenth century. A modern boathouse exists at Cleeve Mill today. Opposite Cleeve Lock is a boathouse, which despite losing its lower section of timbering, is still managing to hold on. Appearing now to be standing on stilts, it is encased in diagonal half-cut timberwork or 'stick' architecture, with leaded casement windows, decorative barge-boards, a tiled roof and terracotta finials. The boarding originally came down to river level, providing full cover for the boats. It is believed to have been built before 1900, and belonged to the Telford-Simpson family, owners of a property called The Temple. An early Frith photograph, dated 1904, shows the boathouse attached to the Temple. The Goring and Streatley Regatta used to hold its prize-giving on the lawns of the house, 'a pretty ornate summer residence' where Mrs Telford-Simpson, no doubt, gave out the prizes.[101] Later owners included Rupert Brooke of Brooke Bond tea, and Pete Townsend of the rock group, The Who. There are plans to restore the boathouse, which is largely unused today.

Approaching Goring is a particularly fine example of the neo-Tudor. On a brick base, with a substantial Tudor chimney, sturdy half-timbering, a decorative balcony, diamond-patterned glazing and gable windows, it sports a foliate decoration of extremely high calibre to its gable and cross beam. It is rural England at its best, with a history that only enhances its appearance. It was built, c. 1890s, for the twentieth Earl of Shrewsbury and Talbot - the founder of Talbot Motors – as a boathouse for his mistress.[102] Its name, Cariad, is Welsh for loved one or darling. A team of 100 builders built a grandiose neo-Tudor mansion with landscaped gardens, waterfall and the boathouse for the Earl. The house was demolished in the early 1970s, but the boathouse remained and was later converted to residential use.[103] Salter's Guide to the Thames notes that in 1913 there were two boathouses in front of the riverside mansion.[104]

Pevsner, writing, in the early 1970s, describes Goring as 'attractively situated at the foot of wooded hill beside the Thames with a wooden bridge and a weir. The village remained small until the Edwardian riverside developments: 'gabled boathouses with balconies and several rich private houses' were built. 'A fast train to London has accelerated the damage'.[105] In fact it is greatly due to the railways, as discussed earlier, that so many of the nineteenth-century boathouses were built on the river; Pevsner seems to be criticising such development. The Howgate boathouse featured in the early photograph stands close to the Cariad boathouse, is of the same period, and has a stained-glass window in it, commemorating the Hudson Bay Company.

Height is no bad thing in a boathouse. It adds dignity, is useful to create further floors, and most importantly to escape the problems of flooding. The Nuns' Acre boathouse has all of this, with clap-board sides, and a balustraded balcony with a long rear elevation. The boathouse has an interesting history. It is believed to date from the 1890s, when it was built with brick foundations, probably on wooden piles, with stud-framing and cladding. Salter's Guide to the Thames notes that Mr. F. C. Strick was the owner in 1913.[106] It is 20m in depth, being built specifically for a Thames steamer. A ventilation unit, in the shape of a dovecote, is still visible today to the rear of the boathouse; the stack of the steamer lay under the dovecote when it was in the dock. The boathouse is believed to have belonged to a large house, which was built on the site of a former nunnery; neither the house nor the nunnery any longer exists. However the connection to the nunnery remains, as a part of the boathouse. An escape tunnel for the clergy, probably used in the sixteenth century, has its end in the boathouse; this has now been blocked up. Local hearsay says that the tunnel was connected to the former Augustinian Nunnery situated to the north side of Goring.

6.25 The Cariad Boathouse
John Clarke 2005

6.26 The Nuns' Acre Boathouse

John Clarke 2005

Close to Goring Lock is a particularly special timbered and thatched boathouse, now converted to domestic living, with French doors opening out onto a full width balcony, with its dock below. The thatched boathouse was originally two buildings, believed to have been built c. 1895. The building had a dry boat storage area beyond the wet dock, and is thought to have been used commercially until the 1960s. The photograph shows the Saunders' boathouses at Goring with their distinctive seven gables and balcony, built by S. E. Saunders in the 1890s, with the thatched boathouse beyond, before its current restoration. Hobbs of Henley purchased the buildings in 1908 for boat building, and the hiring of boats; today the moorings and terraced buildings are rented out. Saunders started their business in the Goring area in 1830, and later moved to the Isle of Wight, where the company became world-renowned for the manufacture of flying boats and hovercraft. Directly opposite, before the lock is the Swan Diplomat Hotel; John Leyland shows a picture of The Swan at Streatley, with its boathouse, in the late nineteenth century.[107]

A row of hidden boathouses, one covered with a tarpaulin, another completely camouflaged by foliage, relieve the sometimes overworked appearance of some boathouses on the next stretch. A simple rustic boathouse stood just before Coombe Park, near the site of the Gatehampton Ferry.[108] A local historian, J.E. Farr, writes that 'between 1907 and 1949 there were seven licences granted by the Thames Commissioners to various individuals to have seven boathouses in the creek behind the cottage. These boathouses gradually fell into disrepair and collapsed. By the late 1950s there was only one boathouse standing which belonged to Mrs G.H. Cholmley of Gatehampton House.'[109] Today the Coombe Park Boathouse is the only one on this stretch of the river. It has the look of a cottage orné, with a balanced composition of two gables, the wet boathouse being central, with fine water-gates; it has an accompanying dry boat house, with skiff roller, under the smaller gable and an octagonal loggia to the opposite elevation. A 1913 Ordnance Survey map shows the Coombe Park Boathouse complete with a 'boathouse walk' in the grounds. *The Building News* of 1892 features a drawing and description of the boathouse; it was built for Mr John Foster of Coombe Park. It is described as being 'situated in one of the most picturesque spots on the banks of the river Thames...and consists of an ample dry boathouse, as well as the dock, a summer-house and tea and dressing-rooms'. It was built to the designs of Mr W. Ravenscroft of Reading.[110] The current owners have plans for its refurbishment.

6.28 The Coombe Park Boathouse

The RIBA Photographs Collection *The Building News* 1892

6.29 The Coombe Park Boathouse

John Clarke 2005

6.30 The Old Swan Boathouse
John Clarke 2005

Whitchurch Lock at Pangbourne follows. The Edwardian landscape at Pangbourne is memorable for the 'Seven Deadly Sins', the great Edwardian mansions which line the Thames on Shooter's Hill, as it approaches the village. The railway, which came to the area in 1840, runs directly behind the houses. The Pangbourne College Boathouse, on the river's edge, is easily recognisable as an institutional building; it is a simple brick structure with a tiled roof. Founded in 1917, the college trained boys for both the Merchant and the Royal Navy; so sailing and rowing were therefore part of the curriculum, but rowing in 'fine boats' was not introduced until 1955. Pangbourne ceased to be a nautical college in 1968, and is now an independent school retaining strong connections with water sports.

In Pangbourne itself, between the somewhat crowded houses on the riverbank, is an inspired example of 'tin-shack' architecture. As a dry boathouse, it stands in splendid serenity, complete with a corrugated iron veranda protecting its wooden construction. Today it is used as the kitchens for the Old Swan Pub, and on a sunny day is as near as the Thames gets to the Caribbean. The Swan boathouse was well known in the vicinity and is often mentioned in accounts of the river. A photograph, dated 1887, shows the building belonging to the Swan Hotel.[111] It is documented that there was a wharf beside the Swan Hotel with 'another wharf and boatyard just upstream from Whitchurch

Bridge' which now no longer exists.[112] Readers of *Three Men in a Boat* will remember that the Swan Inn was journey's end for the adventure, where Jerome describes 'three figures, followed by a shamed-looking dog might have been seen creeping stealthily from the boat-house at the 'Swan', towards the railway station', the rain and poor weather conditions having got the better of them on the return leg of their journey.[113] Interestingly the Swan boathouse is the only boathouse mentioned in Jerome's anecdotal trip down the Thames. Pangbourne did have other boathouses. Two others were used as locations for celebrations in the village: Mr E. T. Ashley's shed in his boatyard was used for Queen Victoria's Golden Jubilee celebrations, and for her Diamond celebrations a Mr Webb lent 'The Boat House' which 'was transformed into a dining room bedecked with flags and flowers for the 500 guests'.[114] *Salter's Guide to the Thames* tells of another boathouse (no longer in existence) 'at the foot of the iron toll bridge is Mr Thomas' house Thames Bank, with a lawn and boathouse fronting the river'.[115]

6.31 The Shanty
John Clarke 2005

The river slows everything down: people idle, moor up, dream, talk, eat and drink. It's a lateral world where you enter a lock, sink, and rise up again to a new panorama, never quite knowing what's round the corner.

Mapledurham Lock with its picturesque mill and house have their own special lure. The 1914 Ordnance Survey map shows a boathouse close to Mapledurham, which no longer appears to exist. After Mapledurham close to a stretch called The Fishery the artist G.D. Leslie described 'a quaintly built modern boat-house on the [Oxfordshire] shore, the room over the water being very prettily conceived'.[116] The quintessential rustic charm of the thatched-balcony boathouse is represented by The Shanty c. 1905, further down this reach on The Warren. Standing on brick base with boat moored within, the upper wooden structure is painted a clotted-cream colour. A rustic poled veranda shelters a pair of French doors; these are protected by a fringe of thatching above which, in the gable, sits a tiny diamond glazed window. This is sweetie-pie land, it has none of the glitz of some of the lower reach boathouses, it is rural England by the water, unspoilt and totally endearing.

6.32 Isomer, The Warren, Caversham
The Oxfordshire County Council Photographic Archive c. 1987

6.33 1900s Boathouses at Caversham, Reading
Berkshire Record Office c. 1900s

The grand turreted, red brick Edwardian presence of Isomer, built c. 1902 for Marie Folliott on The Warren provides the 'wow' factor on this journey down the Thames. In the nineteenth century Henry Taunt noted that 'At Caversham a number of new villa residences are springing up at Caversham Hill, along the pretty Mapledurham Road'; the smart appendage of a boathouse was the inevitable accompaniment.[117] The area was described at the time as 'Reading's Richmond'.[118] The Edwardian Baroque of The Warren dominates this stretch of the river with its polygonal turret, cupola belvedere, Tudor gable and large integral boathouse. With panoramic fenestration on two floors of the turret, frontal balconies and a balustrade to the upper section of the belvedere, the occupants of this riverside mansion must have felt a deep sense of integration with their watery surroundings.

An early postcard shows that this reach was, around the 1900s, positively brimming with boathouses, large and small, including the stunning broad-gabled example to the forefront of the card. Although the image is slightly blurred, the balcony appears to be supported by two extravagant marine caryatids. The 1914 Ordnance Survey map shows ten boathouses on this reach at the time.

ON THE THAMES AT CAVERSHAM, READING

6.34 The Balihoo Boathouse
Jeremy Paxton 2005

An exciting modern house, with an integral dock, follows. This sets a standard for contemporary boathouse building on the Thames, being the winner of the *Daily Telegraph* House of the Year, and of an RIBA Downland prize in 1999. It is rare accolade for a Thames boathouse. It is constructed of red brick with an open dock below. The house shows symmetrically balanced steel spiral staircases to each side, winding their way up to the first floor, with a full-width balcony, from which the current owners dive into the Thames. The gable is clad with wood-facing, with centrally set French windows, with a small upper balcony. The structure integrates well with the river, proving that contemporary domestic architecture need not always follow the ubiquitous neo-Tudor. It can be red brick, meaningful and modern. An earlier boathouse, apparently of a modernist design, existed on the site; as a young boy the current owner put a card through the boathouse letterbox; twenty years on the owners

telephoned him to see if he was still interested in purchasing the site. The result is the Balihoo Boathouse.

Reading Rowing Club's barn-type structure, with its generous window span and 'X' framed balcony running along the length of the building, seems a popular place, close to Caversham Bridge, for both rowers and swans. The building is owned by Reading Borough Council, and let to the club on a peppercorn rent; its internal arrangements are apparently plagued with design problems. Of substantial proportions, its tiled roof span is a notable feature as you pass over the bridge. In the nineteenth century Henry Taunt's guide recorded that T. Freebody housed boats at Caversham, on the Oxfordshire shore.[119]

Industry is never far away on the Thames. At Algoa Wharfe, in the late nineteenth century, close to Caversham Bridge, was the large industrial site of the barge builders, R. Talbot & Sons. The boatbuilding company of Easts also had their headquarters in the town. Reading today is no longer a centre for boat builders, but has become the Thames valley centre for hi-tech and computer companies.[120] The 1914 maps of Reading show that the town had four boathouses on its banks.[121]

East's main boathouse was situated at Caversham, just above the lock. They housed and repaired 'gentlemen's boats', and also 'organised riverside concerts'. By 1898 they had expanded their business to Sandhurst, and were even opening a 'depôt on the Seine.'[122] In the 1920s Reading Bridge was built in between the two sets of boathouses in the picture.

6.35 East's Boat Building Company, Reading

Reading Library 1902

2177. The old Mill, Shiplake.

The run up to Henley starts after Caversham Lock, through Dreadnought Reach to Sonning Bridge, where Bluecoat's School has its own utilitarian steel shed. Jerome K. Jerome, on his journey up the Thames, described the stretch from Sonning to Shiplake – he was going upstream to Oxford – as 'very placid, hushed, and lonely'; the Thames Valley Business Park, on the perimeter of Reading, which houses the computer giants Microsoft and Oracle, has dramatically changed the landscape today, but there is still, after Reading, an essential element of the wildness that Jerome describes.[123] For the Victorian adventurer, Sonning was 'The most fairy-like little nook on the whole river'; today it is still a picturesque Thames-side village.[124] The Bull pub remains, according to Jerome purists, an atmospheric overnight river-stop. The Sonning reach is not however the most prolific for boathouses, but from Shiplake onwards things pick up; a 1900s picture of the Old Mill at Shiplake shows that the simplest shed on water served its purpose in providing aquatic cover. Such a building is almost lost into the background of the working mill; the mill at Goring had a similar arrangement. Further down the river Shiplake Court, now Shiplake College was built c. 1905 by the architect Ernest George (1839-1922) for the stockbroker Robert Harrison, in the neo-Tudor style. The boathouse is now used by the school.[125] On this reach too was the boathouse to Shiplake House, situated close to Phillimore's Island.[126] The 1932 Ordnance Survey map shows nine boathouses in total in the Shiplake area, with five further downstream at Wargrave. Interestingly the numbers are pretty much the same today.

The Shiplake College Boathouse is sited on a great bend in the river. The school's boating complex is fronted by the neo-Tudor boathouse, with a collection of purpose-built modern sheds behind. The chalk cliffs make a dramatic backdrop. A wooden foot bridge sits to the fore of the boathouse, with the water-gates visible below. The boathouse has French windows to its river-room; the school's crest with the nameplate showing 'Shiplake College Boathouse' sits in the gable.

A variety of boathouses follow, including an attractive aqua-coloured clap-board boathouse, with a New England, Cape Cod air to it, sitting quietly by Shiplake Lock. This wooden building was put up around 1910; an article in *House and Garden* by George Drower (1990) shows an earlier photograph.[127] The boathouse has recently been renovated with new sheet-piling and a shuttered boat entrance. It has retained its gabled structure, balcony and French windows.

Wargrave Boating Club has two simple white boatsheds; a little further in a small backwater there are more boathouses, the most prominent is a neo-Tudor pebbledash and brick, with a bay window, opening out onto a generous balcony, decorated with ball finials. The clap-board boat storage is below. Contrasts in boat house building are great; the white 'carport' boathouse alongside, and the neo-Tudor, both serve their purpose.

Close by is a brick and tiled gabled boathouse belonging to Ferry House, with a clock tower and miniature cupola; it has a rather discreet version of the 'up-and-over' garage door. This is a dry boathouse, with a deep slipway, containing tracks for running the boats. The present building replaced an earlier 1950s boathouse which was destroyed in a storm; it has been used by the same family for the last 22 years. The use of the up-and-over garage door establishes a new boathouse type on this most prestigious of reaches. Red brick editions are to be found on many parts of the Thames today, often with carriage lamps, simply converting the role of the garage to the water. Whilst not to everybody's taste, the adaptation of use is interesting, and its place cannot be ignored in the boathouse genre. The property also has a fully-functional wet boathouse.

7.4 Val Wyatt's Boathouse
Jack Wyatt c. 1940s

Val Wyatt's boatyard dates back to 1845, when the family ran the George and Dragon, the ferry and their boat business from the pub at Wargrave. William Wyatt's son, Francis is listed as a professional fisherman in Henry Taunt's guide to the Thames of 1872. In the early 1930s, having given up the lease at the George and Dragon, the Wyatts bought a property called The Willows half a mile downstream from the pub, along with the adjoining meadow. The Willows was the first house in Wargrave to have electric light. The property also had an old cedar shingled boathouse, which was eventually used as a store for the expanding business. The first boatshed was built in the 1930s; the whole family helped cart away the clay, which had to be dug out for the concrete walls. The boatyard was eventually sold by the Wyatt family in 1976; the present company still trades under the Wyatt name. The timbered boathouse to The Willows is used as an office, with a wet boathouse area leading to dry storage beyond. It is made of cedar boarding with first-floor French windows, a timber balcony and has a hipped gable.

Further on, before the bend, a substantial pair of semi-detached houses, with impressive Tudor chimneys dominate the river. Heavy brackets support an expansive balcony, with the wet-boat access below. The fenestration runs the full width of the first floor of each house; the second floor has recessed verandas. The latter have been infilled with modern glazing. There is no doubt that this façade was designed with its aquatic surroundings in mind. The house is pebble-dashed, with heart motifs cut in the wood-work, reminiscent of the work of the architect Charles Voysey (1857-1941). The building was designed c. 1900 as two separate houses; River Home stands to the left and Green Pastures to the right. Four generations of one family have lived in River Home, having connections with both houses since the 1930s. There was previously a substantial third boathouse adjoining Green Pastures, which was burnt down in the 1930s. This belonged to a property called Thatched Holme; it was accessed over a small bridge, which has now gone.

Further on a brick and tile boathouse, with substantial wooden brackets, and a gently splayed tiled roof is deceptive from the river. It takes the eye the full length of its interior to leaded diamond lights at the rear. The owners believe that the boathouse originally belonged to Bolney Court, which is next door, and was built around 1905. The 1926 Ordnance Survey Map shows boathouses opposite Bolney Court. The boathouse was originally of timber construction with clap-board facings. The early timber foundations have been renewed with concrete and brick, saving as many original timbers as possible. The hand-made clay roof tiles are original, and the doors are in the process of being restored. The boathouse was built specifically for a steam launch and a pair of punts. There were four vents in the roof for the steam and smoke to escape, and the rear section was and is still ramped with two rows of wooden rollers, to facilitate moving the punts in and out of the boathouse. The White House, built by George Walton for George Davison, the

managing director of Eastman Kodak, the photographic company, stands close by. The RIBA hold a drawing of 'the landing stage for mooring the 'log cabin' houseboat' to the White House.[128] The 1932 O.S. map shows another boathouse close to the White House.

The boathouses on this reach have an extremely interesting lineage. In the late nineteenth century, when the railway came to the area, houseboat owners were drawn to the banks along the Bolney Road area – the road itself was not yet built – as a suitable mooring place. Before the station was built, the trains had to be waved down, as there was no designated stopping point. Houseboats became a familiar part of the scene; the backwater of the Lashbrook, being used as their winter storage. Gradually the odd house sprang up from the houseboat settlement, followed by boathouses, until the present colony of large houses and boathouses came into being.

An important commercial boathouse on this reach, immediately downstream of the Lashbrook, was that of the East Boat Building Company, built in 1899. The company's main premises were on the south side of Reading Bridge, on the site of the new Thames Water building.[129] The East's Shiplake building was constructed from bricks taken from an old Reading mill. In the late nineteenth century boaters would take the train down from London to Shiplake, to hire their skiff at Easts. The company even had a private right of way from the station at Shiplake. The company name still advertises itself to train-goers, from the roof tiles of the rear elevation. The boathouse had eight changing rooms and two bathrooms; this was a necessary facility as the men all changed into white flannels for boating. Today the property is used as a private boathouse, and is immaculately maintained.

7.5 The East Boat Building Company

Shiplake c. 1900

7.6 The 'Vanderbilt' Boathouse
John Clarke 2005

The mock Tudor never really disappears on the Thames. Hidden by willows, we find a little timbered skiff house, open-ended chalet boathouses, and a substantial dry boatshed on this part of the river; all create on-going variety for the river-rambler. Luxury too is a consistent feature on this substantial Shiplake to Henley reach. A large half-timbered property, built in the late nineteenth century by the American Vanderbilt family, boasts not two but three boathouses: one a substantial timbered version on brick, with a picture window to the river, and the second a more utilitarian affair, called the 'centre deck'; its lower entrance is draped in ivy with a glazed cabin and a sundeck on ground level. The third is a dry boathouse, which has an early-twentieth-century heated swimming pool, whose water was heated from an overhead tank. *Salter's Guide to the Thames* describes how the main stream, running parallel [to the Hennerton backwater] 'is distinguished by a long line of houseboats...conspicuous among them is Mr. A. G. Vanderbilt's *Venture*, perhaps the most luxurious houseboat in the world', built by Salters in 1909.[130]

A little further downstream is a haven of four boathouses, all built around the same period. The first, Eyot Wood, is a substantial half-timbered house c. 1920s with wooden balconies and an integral wet dock; it originally had a 'dance' room over the dock area, reflecting the passion for dancing in the 1920s. Alongside, is the smaller property 'Dabchick', which has an integral dry dock, used only for light boats. The properties of 'Dabchick' and 'Little Grebe' - the third house - were originally one. A boathouse stood on the plot of 'Little Grebe'; this was originally the boathouse for 'Dabchick'. 'Little Grebe' was completed in 2004, on a tight plot where, at the turn of the century, visiting boats could moor. It is a contemporary timbered design with its wooden decking projecting out, to make cover for the boats moored below. The fourth boathouse in this quartet is a simple white wooden building, built around 1900, with a projecting and enclosed viewing area, under which is the wet dock. Last but not least in this little group is the ubiquitous 'up-and-over' garage boathouse with a very smart clay-tile roof. A mile and a half up river on the opposite bank is the Lodden, about which local folklore rather strangely warns that 'anyone who swims against [it will] feel...sick'.[131]

After Marsh Lock on the Berkshire bank a little wooden bridge protects what appears to be a rather unprepossessing boathouse, sitting shyly beside a vermiculated cottage orné, with distinctive circular glazing to its windows. This belongs to Park Place. Venture closer and you will see this is one of Henley's jewels. An ornate Victorian cast iron frame supports a shallow corrugated iron roof. Internally it is a delight, with decorated brackets and posts. Hopefully its owners recognise that it deserves to be preserved.

As the river approaches Henley we enter the 'Las Vegas' strip of boathouse building. The estate at Park Place chose to decorate their 'very pretty Gothic' boathouse with extensive half-timbering, an oriel bay, a notable bressummer beam and the most elaborate of barge-boarding, which originally had a central finial post.[132] The Tudor arch of the boathouse is hewn from rough cast stone, giving it a defensive air. A bearded mascaron sits to the head of the arch, presumably placed as a river deity.[133] Park Place has recently been sold for the highest price ever for an estate on the Thames, and is due to be extensively restored.

7.7 Park Place Boathouse, Henley

English Heritage NMR c. 1945-80

Pevsner writes that the house (Park Place) was designed by Thomas Cundy in 1870, in what he claimed to be a 'rather dreary French Renaissance' style; Pevsner deemed the principal 'interest of Park Place is its grounds as beautified by General Conway, who bought the estate in 1752.' Conway erected the Cyclopic Bridge (1781-6) in what is known rather endearingly as Happy Valley, and a grotto with 'six tunnel-vaulted entries'. He also mentions the 'pretty early nineteenth-century cottage with barge boarded gables which was built as a boathouse'.[134] Somewhat ignominiously this seemingly grand appendage to Park Place has the local name of Underpants Boathouse; with imagination local residents see the shape of a rather large pair of underpants, which seem to have developed from the pebble-dashed side elevation. *The Guide to Henley* 1826 has a long description of the grounds and attractions at Park Place, but there is no mention of a boathouse.[135] The estate had just been bought by E. Fuller Maitland M.P. in 1825. The second edition, 1838, reports 'Mr Maitland has built a very handsome Boat House in the Elizabethan style'. Leyland also writes

'The boat-house of Park Place is a charming feature of the reach, though some have found fault with its artificial character. Yet it is more than a boat-house. It is a pretty little riverside dwelling...the charm of its high gables – one of them crowned with a cross – its picturesque barge boards, and the saints in the niches below them, all with a background of the most delicious foliage'. The saints who stood in the large boathouse niche and in the two smaller niches on the cottage gables have disappeared; the religious significance of the statues and a cross to the gable is unusual iconography for a Thames boathouse. His critique of its artificial character probably refers to the rather whimsical neo-Tudor architecture of the boathouse, and perhaps also to the religious iconography. The neo-Tudor style was in vogue by the later nineteenth-century; it appears that the boathouse was built by 1838, when architects would have been more likely to choose either a classical or a Gothic mode.[136]

7.8 The Hybrid Sunroom-Boathouse

John Clarke 2005

Marsh Lock separates Park Place from the town. Above the lock, on the opposite bank, is a thatched boathouse c. 1900s, which was once owned by the actress Beatrice Lillie. This is followed, amongst others upstream of the lock by a hybrid boathouse: half sunroom and half wet boathouse, which has been innovatively constructed from a timber-framed shed.

About one hundred yards downstream of Marsh Lock there is a white boathouse with a Scandinavian feel to it, which has wet boat storage below. It has a prominent white balcony, full-width French windows, with a small oeil-de-boeuf, or round window, set within the boarded gable. It was built in the 1900s as a boathouse for the Mill owner, who lived in Marsh Mills House.[137] Close to it is a salmon-pink timbered boathouse, with a slatted water-gate, wooden 'X' patterned balcony, and a miniature oriel window set high into the gable.

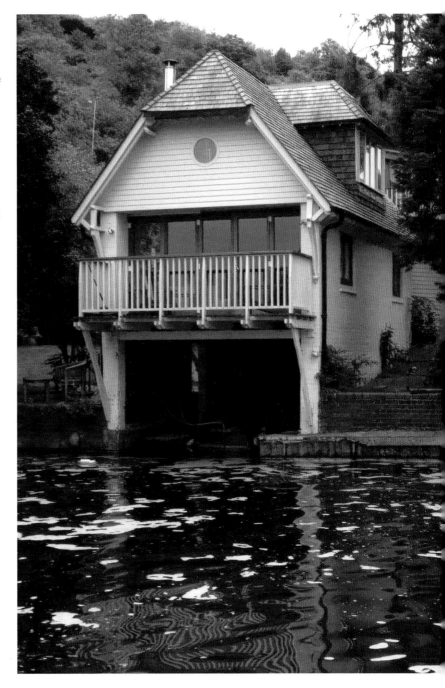

7.10 The Carpenter's Arms and Boathouses at Henley Bridge
Henley Royal Regatta c. 1980s

7.11 The Henley Royal Regatta Headquarters
Henley Royal Regatta c. 1987

Approaching Henley Bridge, on the Berkshire side were two substantial boathouses which the picture alongside shows, the one on the left belonged to The Carpenter's Arms. Both show simple timber cladding. The site is occupied today by Terry Farrell's essay in post-modernism, the Henley Royal Regatta Headquarters, opened in 1986. The upper floor is the Secretary's flat, the offices are at ground level, and the boat storage below. The building was opened by the Queen in 1986, and was the winner of several design awards, including an RIBA Regional Award in 1988.[138] Standing on a 'high battered-brick plinth' its architecture is a play on classicism: the pediment, the orders, the cornice and the dentil.[139] Circles, triangles, rectangles and squares are simplified to large brightly coloured shapes, whilst glass, red brick and decorative stone-work give the building its integral dignity. The use of the pediment and red brick reflect Henley's eighteenth-century architecture, and the marriage of a Venetian window into the pediment is post-modern pastiche at its best.[140] The substantial wet dock below has elaborate iron gates; this houses slipper launches and other necessities for the smooth running of the Regatta. The building was described by the journalist, Colin Amery, as 'small but prestigious...[standing] by the...bridge like a new temple, strangely proportioned but ingeniously planned;' it is affectionately known in the town as 'The Temple to Rowing'.[141] The choice of such an avant-garde architect of the time is proof that artistry and innovation can be successfully embraced and integrated into a small and historical English market town. The plans of the building illustrate the three working levels of the Headquarters, with the prestigious committee room housed in the apex of the pediment, overlooking the river.

7.12 The HRR Committee Room

Henley Royal Regatta Richard Bryant and Arcaid Picture Library 1986

From the Middle Ages Henley was an important trading centre, being the farthest navigable point upstream for barge traffic during the summer months, when the river was running low. Hilaire Belloc writes how Henley's early bridge, dating from this time, gave the town its strategic importance.[142] Boatbuilding was important to the town's commercial status; wharfs and boathouses would have been a familiar part of its architectural make-up. One of the biggest surprises at Henley to those familiar with today's panorama is that the whole range of the former Little White Hart Hotel 'c. 1890 and gabled and half-timbered, with wooden balconies', was simply a very large boathouse for the Red Lion Hotel, with the hotel bar alongside.[143] A wide variety of boats was available, launches for hire and boats to let, as the photograph shows. Today the Boathouse and the adjoining pedimented building have been remodelled into shops, cafes and flats.[144]

Leander Club, the epi-centre of competitive rowing, with its clubrooms and integral dry boathouse, stands just after Henley Bridge on the Berkshire shore. Its origins go back to 1818, when the club first had its 'quarters...at Searle's Yard at Stangate, alias Lambeth...upstream from Westminster Bridge', now the site of St Thomas' Hospital. By 1866 the Club started the process of 'erecting a large and expensive Boathouse and Clubrooms on the Banks of the Thames at Putney', next to the London Rowing Club. By 1887 the club had an enclosure on Temple Island at Henley for the annual Regatta, and from the summer of 1892 they rented rooms for the month at the Royal Hotel, Henley which provided a clubroom. By 1896 a scheme was underway to build a permanent clubhouse and boathouse in the town. Their present clubhouse was built the following year with 'ordinary club accommodation...[to include] a Ladies' dining-room and a Ladies' water closet, as well as sleeping accommodation for twenty-one members', the funding having been raised by a members' entrance fee. The club is known as 'The Pink Palace' in reference to the distinctive Leander pink club colour, really a salmon pink, worn by its members. In 1997 a centenary appeal for funds was inaugurated by the Club. This was coupled with a generous sum from the Lottery Sports Fund. It enabled the club to provide high-tech gym, medical and physiotherapy facilities for both men and its newly elected women members, along with its extensive dining and clubrooms.[145]

7.13 The Red Lion Hotel Boathouse

The Oxfordshire County Council Photographic Archive c. 1890s

7.14 The Wharfe Lane Boathouses
The Oxfordshire County Council Photographic Archive c. 1890s

7.15 The Wharfe Lane Boathouses
John Clarke 2008

Two hundred metres down, on the town side, at the junction of
Thameside and New Street, the distinctive range of 'late
Victorian boat-houses with gables and ornamental bargeboards,'
shows a hive of domestic activity.[146] Low spanning gables,
decorated with barge-boards and balconies, form a continuous
range of five boathouses. These boathouses were built by Hobbs
in 1892, on the site of the Old Commercial Wharf, known as
Webb's Wharf. The wharf stretched from New Street to Phyllis
Court; it was demolished in 1866. Tony Hobbs writes that 'many
boats were built in the lower level boathouses and the upper
levels were rented out for holiday and residential premises.'
Hobbs later built their present boathouse on Station Road in
1898. Both premises were in use commercially until the 1930s,
when the company transferred their business to Station Road
and the Wharfe Lane property was sold off as private housing.

7.16 Water's Edge, The Dragon Brackets

Nigel Chapman Photography 2006

7.17 Water's Edge, The Terracotta Dragon

Nigel Chapman Photography 2006

Two other boathouses stand next to the Wharfe Lane five. The most distinctive, Water's Edge has a first-floor sexagonal tower, with a pyramidal roof, heavy glazing, imposing round-headed water-gates, and extensive half-timbering. Its heavy black and gold brackets, with their distinctive dragons and foliate decoration, are particularly notable. A well-muscled terracotta dragon sits on the gable, enhancing the 'dragon' boathouse theme. Water's Edge was built in 1893 for 'the rich solicitor' Sir Frank Crisp, the owner of the fantastical Gothic mansion, Friar Park (1896). A rockery, created from the stone used at Friar Park, covers the side-wall of the garden at Water's Edge. Friar Park stands high above the town, and was the home of the late Beatle, George Harrison.[147] Local hearsay goes that Harrison was disappointed that the boathouse was, by then, not part of the estate when he bought Friar Park. His posthumous album notably featured the track 'I'm a Pisces man and the river runs through my soul'. The boathouse has a 26m wet dock, and its upper floor has undoubtedly the best view of the Henley Regatta course.[148] It is now divided into two properties, the ground floor being originally the dry boathouse, beside the wet dock. Next door is a pair of semi-detached timbered boathouses, with gables. The end boathouse of this pair has a distinctive square sentinel box to its side, which similarly must give a great view down the Regatta course.

Just before the Remenham Rowing Club, on the Berkshire shore, is a large boathouse, which belongs to the wooden dacha of Barn Elms. It has a towpath bridge, but the boathouse itself is hidden by foliage and willows. Barn Elms belonged to the actress Gladys Cooper, but the boathouse is a modern addition, c. 1998, built by Peter Freebody. The Upper Thames Rowing Club sits close by. On the same bank stood the old Boom Boathouse, where the booms brought out annually for the Regatta were stored. This no longer exists. The 1926 Ordnance Survey Map shows a boathouse near Remenham Lodge, and also the Fawley Court Boathouse. An early photograph shows a simple shed boathouse, on the downstream Oxfordshire bank, with accommodation above; this is believed to have been the Fawley Court boathouse, which no longer exists, but was featured on Henry Taunt's map of the Regatta Course.[149] On the same bank, further downstream, the Henley Management College has a functional wet boathouse of wooden construction, believed to have been built in the mid-nineteenth century, but restored in 1993, which stands in stark contrast to its classical setting. The boathouse appears on the Ordnance Survey map of 1876.

At Hambleden Lock the backwater holds an agrarian pair of timber, hipped, clay-tiled boathouses. These sit behind the weir, with open, slatted water-gates. They were owned by the Smith family at Hambleden, descendants of the newsagent W.H. Smith. The present owners bought them from Harry Hambleden, about twenty-five years ago. At the time they were completely overgrown; the roof and doors have since been replaced.

Close by a boathouse has been innovatively created from a stone bridge, built around fifty years ago. Opposite the Hambleden Mill, in the late nineteenth century, stood a small rustic boathouse, which no longer exists; the Ordnance Survey map of 1926 shows four boathouses in the lock area.[150] The artist G. D. Leslie confirms that' behind Hambleden Lock, in the waters leading to the mill, Mr Schwabe's boat-house and little fleet of sailing cutters may be seen; the boatman's cottage adjoining was formerly a small inn'.[151] The stretch above the lock was popular for sailing in the late nineteenth century.

Further down the river, opposite the Ferry crossing to the Flower Pot pub, is one of the Thames' classics, a castellated wet boathouse of sizeable proportions whose turrets and arched entrance drip with ivy. Standing beside an Edwardian house, long since divided, this is neo-Tudor architecture at its most theatrical.

Passing the imposing eighteenth-century classicism of Culham Court, sitting high on the hill overlooking the Thames, Leyland reminds us that 'there is an extremely pretty backwater with the picturesque boathouse of Culham Court' on this reach. The artist G.D. Leslie also mentions the boathouse, with 'a pretty little cottage and garden attached.'[152] Although the backwater remains, the boathouse is no longer there.[153]

The village of Medmenham today has only one simple boathouse on its banks; the 1926 Ordnance Survey map shows a boathouse close to Medmenham Abbey, and one other, upstream on the opposite bank. A little further on the magnificent cliff-top neo-Tudor court that is Danesfield House, now a hotel and spa, was built on the site of a former mansion, between 1899 and 1901. Sale documents reveal that, in 1895, the estate boasted 'Two Picturesque Summer Houses, well sheltered with uninterrupted prospects and lower down, a Large Rustic House or Tea Room with thatched roof having broad eaves sheltering a balcony'. More importantly there is reference to a 'Capital Boat House, a wood and tiled building with brick foundations', believed to have been situated on the site of the RAF Sailing Club at Medmenham. No photograph has been found, but its existence is confirmed on the early maps.[154]

At Medmenham too, the architect Sir Reginald Blomfield RA (1856-1942) designed a boathouse for Wittington House, the grand neo-classical house (1898-1899) built in the Queen Anne style for the International Store owner, Hudson Ewbanke Kearley, 1st Earl of Devonport.[155] Kearley was a Member of Parliament and Chairman of the Port of London Authority. He was responsible for the building of Wittington and its magnificent grounds, which included a world-renowned rockery in the under-cliff, a steep chalk escarpment by the river. This was featured in *Country Life* of 1927.[156] In his memoirs he describes the boathouse location: 'Leaving the water garden and turning our steps eastward towards the house, we reach the boathouse and a gardener's cottage, an agreeable little red brick house, pleasantly situated by the side of a stream'.[157] The grounds also feature a flint and brick pump-house, the earliest flash lock capstan on the river, and other services essential to the 1900s estate. Kearley took great interest in the architecture of the grounds. 'Across the stream at points...I have thrown little bridges of concrete faced with a mosaic of flints, of which there is a superabundance at Wittington, for the concrete weathers rapidly and soon provides a hold for moss and other tiny plants.'[158]

The boathouse was a dry boathouse, with access for skiffs; the original steel joists for the floor are still evident. It is built of red brick with a stone band course and chamfered quoins of Ham Hill stone, echoing those of the main house. It has a hipped pyramid roof, originally topped by a wooden finial, with a deeply-emphasised dentil cornice, an elongated chimney, and generous square balcony with stone balls sitting to each corner. Its rear elevation has a pair of square sashes with a simple side entrance. The river front shows a range of sashes broken by an arched doorcase, with emphasised wooden keystone, giving the semblance of a Serlian window, opening out onto the balcony and the river beyond. Internally there are two small rooms with

fireplaces, one the picnic-room overlooking the river, and the other for domestic purposes.[159] The water-gate access is also arched, and decorated with a stone keystone; a brick staircase gives access from the land. The boathouse's orientation over the Hurley backwater is exceptional. Describing himself as a 'keen river man' Kearley wrote in his memoirs: 'one can look down on to a part of Hurley Weir which forms a great crescent of foaming white, on which the light of the sun sparkles and plays in summer-time, and whose murmur is never stilled all the year round'.[160] Such was the setting for his rock garden 'my chief task and also my chief pleasure' and for his idyllic boathouse close by. Interestingly too, Jerome K. Jerome writes how, by Hurley Weir 'I have often thought that I could stay a month without having sufficient time to drink in all the beauty of the scene'.[161] A nineteenth-century architect-designed boathouse on the Thames is a comparative rarity. To own one such example by a leading Edwardian architect must be a joy. It is symmetrical, playfully acknowledging the rules of classicism, and is light, generously-proportioned and purposeful; the quintessential dolls-house by the river.

At Hurley Lock a backwater reveals a similarly picturesque boathouse, emulating a barn, with a timber frame of half circular and ogee braces.[162] The widely-placed wooden slats, hipped clay-tiled roof and shaped timbers make it particularly distinctive. It was built in 1903-4, and was used, until the 1940s, to house punts for hire. The 1900's landowners had some differences with their neighbours, The Mill House; the boathouse was apparently built out of spite to prevent the Mill House owners having a view upstream. The vernacular rhythm of its composition far supersedes its somewhat difficult origins.

Taunt writes that the remains of an old Benedictine monastery are to be found at Hurley.[163] Close by 'is the old refectory, which was formed into the stables for the mansion built on the site of the old monastery and called, after it, Lady Place.[164] The historian, Peel, writes that the original Lady Place was built by the 'Tudor sea-dog, Sir Richard Lovelace'; it was later replaced by an Edwardian mansion.'[165] The name of the boathouse reflects this local history. The 1926 Ordnance Survey map of the area shows three boathouses on the Thames at Hurley; The artist G.D. Leslie describes the boathouse near the footbridges [presumably at Hurley] which belonged to Sir Gilbert East, as 'not an ugly one...in time it will look very much better, as it is chiefly the varnish which spoils it now'.[166] There has been a decline in the number of boathouses on these upper parts of the Thames. Large estates such as Culham Court and Park Place have changed hands recently; hopefully some boathouses will be restored, and others re-built.

The boatbuilder, Peter Freebody's, boathouse Thames Lodge, c. 1890s, sits within its lake-like backwater, close to Hurley Lock. The Freebody family has been building and storing boats on the Thames for over three hundred years. The boathouse uses half-timbering in its gable, and like many others of its genre has French windows, a balcony, barge-boards, and a clay-tiled roof upon which sits a terracotta dragon finial, poised as a watch guard over the river. The boathouse's existence is particularly pleasing as it is still a working boathouse, somewhat rare today, being surrounded by river craft both old and new in various states of restoration.

Peter Freebody recounts that the original owner of the boathouse was the Reverend Farrer, who built it around 1890, and who also owned Hurley House in the High Street.[167] Peter Freebody's grandfather bought the property in 1933; the boathouse then stood contained within a high weatherboard fence. It had skiffs hanging from four big hooks under the first floor. 'There was also at that time a springboard for diving, which was 'nicely sited on the river landing stage'. 'Upstairs there was just one big room with a balcony overlooking the river [this area of a boathouse is known as 'the social floor'] and one big cupboard for fishing rods'. By 1962 'the upstream side was slipping into the water' this was stabilized and corrected, the roofline was raised and dormer windows put in to make the building into a proper home. In 1968 the boathouse was further extended to give a total length of 16m. The office for the boatyard is now situated at the land-end of the boathouse. Freebody remembers being fascinated as a little boy by 'the very elaborate earth closet in the grounds... next to the boathouse. This comprised, among other things, of a very nicely made metal hopper which contained dry earth which, by using a lever, was dropped periodically over the contents'. He also remarks that the terracotta dragon on the apex of the roof 'has kept watch

over the boathouse for many years'; these clay figures were manufactured at the Maidenhead Brick and Tile company at their Star Works in nearby Knowl Hill. They are a notable feature on many of the Thames boathouses.

Harleyford Manor's wooden boathouse has probably seen better days. The house itself was designed by Sir Robert Taylor in 1755, who also built Maidenhead Bridge. The nineteenth-century painter G.D. Leslie mentions 'a very fine boat-house with the stream running through it, near which a beautiful plane tree overhangs the water' in the Harleyford area.[168] A little further on, past Temple Lock, is a simple wooden shed with tin roof and an aqua up-and-over door. The use of colour in this setting gives the simplest of buildings a painterly edge.

7.23 The Old Bridge House Boathouse

John Clarke 2005

Close by someone with a sense of humour has used a Batley garage with open slatted gates to create his boathouse. Hilaire Belloc published a drawing of the boathouse of Bisham Vicarage, close to the church. This was a simple brick affair, which no longer exists, although it is shown on early maps. An 1889 photograph in *Forgotten Thames* shows another boathouse, with distinctive square-patterned watergates, on the towpath, opposite Higginson Park at Marlow.[169] Taunt's guide lists Meakes and Redknap's Victoria Boat Houses near the Bridge.[170] The Francis Frith collection has a photograph of a boat-letting business in Great Marlow, which is probably the Victoria Boat Houses.[171] The 1923 Ordnance Survey Map shows two boathouses before the bridge at Marlow, one of which was Shaw's, and the other close by the site of the old Marlow Mills, downstream near the lock.[172] Marlow Rowing Club, situated just before Marlow Bridge, was built in 1897, with a brick base and clap-boarding, French doors, balcony and an oeil-de-boeuf (round window) within the gable. A later wider-bayed addition, c. 1970s, sits to its side. The early history of Marlow Rowing Club has a strong connection to the Meakes and Redknap Boat House. The Club was inaugurated at a meeting at the Compleat Angler Hotel in 1871. Initially 'quarters [were found] in the boat-sheds under Marlow Bridge on the Bucks side...[and] a move was [later] made to the boathouse of Messrs. Meakes and Redknap on the opposite side of the river.'[173] This only lasted up to 1892, by which time the club had financial problems. 'Fortunately a temporary way out' was found, by erecting a tent on the land just above Messrs. Meakes and Redknap's boathouse. 'For the next four rowing seasons the club was under canvas.' By 1896 a lease was signed on a site adjoining Marlow Bridge on the Berkshire side for the erection of a boathouse; the current clubhouse was opened in 1897 and the freehold purchased in 1910.[174]

7.24 Thames Lawn Boathouse

John Clarke 2005

Immediately downstream of Marlow Bridge are two other boathouses, belonging to different properties, which create a memorable pair: the first is a brick and flint Romanesque arched building, with a distinctive rounded portcullis gate, a mascaron to the keystone, and decorative stone edging to its facade. It creates an original one-off, with a highly individual shape from its rather 'lean-to' origins. It was built around 1880 and stands on the site of the original Marlow Bridge.[175] The boathouse belongs to the Old Bridge House, which was apparently constructed c. 1875-6 by Thomas Rolls Hoare. Pevsner writes that the builder, in 1860, was a Mr Lovell; [and asks] 'was he also the architect?'[176] The boathouse was originally very shallow and was used for punts and skiffs; it has featured in one or two films.

The second close-by, is now in fact not a boathouse, but is an 'exact copy of the boathouse that was a few yards away'. It makes a heavy play on the diamond and the square, with diamond mock-timbering to its side elevation and gable balanced by an open square-patterned set of water-gates. An early photograph shows the original boathouse to Thames Lawn in Marlow c. 1900s, built in comfortable proximity to the Lodge. It was an open trellis-like affair, using diamond and box patterns with a slate roof, providing adequate cover with generous ventilation.

7.25 Rippling Waters
John Clarke 2006

The river winds on after Marlow Lock. Approaching Winter Hill in a small side-creek, sits one of the river Thames's real beauties, a late-nineteenth-century boathouse. In the summer the building is almost hidden by vast ribbons of green foliage. It is a fantasy boathouse, a Hansel and Gretel affair with high water-gates reaching to just below the first floor balustrade, balanced by two giant pairs of elaborately carved brackets. A wide range of French windows sits in the main gable, whose decorative barge-boards reflect the circular timber patterning within the gable. It is everything a boathouse should be: romantic, flamboyant and secretive. The owners have little knowledge of its history. The 1923 Ordnance Survey Map of the area shows the boathouse and others in the vicinity. A boathouse is shown in close proximity to a house called Green Gables, and others seemingly belonging to Quarry Court, the Lodge, Quarry Wood Hall, and Willow House. It is believed that 'Rippling Waters' may have belonged to a large house, which dominating the hill, called Tall Trees. The boathouse has been a popular choice for the film industry, having featured in *True Blue* and *Wind in the Willows*.

7.26 & 7.27 The Clay Hung and Dragon Boathouses
John Clarke 2005

7.28 The Aqua Trellis Boathouse
John Clarke 2005

Three other notable boathouses exist in this area today. The first has partially open sides, a gently splayed clay-tiled roof, with a clay-tile-hung gable. It sits securely nestling into a high stone wall, below the imposing Edwardian property of Quarry Lodge. Its current owner writes that the boathouse is marked on the 1899 Ordnance Survey, and at the time was part of the property known as Doornfontein, later to be renamed Quarry Court. Doornfontein was owned by the eccentric Baron de Barreto, described rather mysteriously as 'a major benefactor of Belize'. Baron de Barreto had the largest launch on this stretch of the Thames at the time. A sales brochure of the property, dating from 1913, describes how 'Access to the River is gained at the east end of the strip and opposite the lodge is placed the excellent timber and tiled boathouse [17m x 6m] capable of housing launches with landing stage, two rooms over part and a balcony overlooking the river'. The next notable boathouse on this stretch is distinguished by its timbered gable and a terracotta dragon finial, which sits at the head of its long clay-tiled roof. This is followed by a contemporary aqua-painted neo-Gothic boathouse, whose upper walls are filled with a lattice inset, and a barge-board of ornate fretwork.

An unidentified image of a house and boathouse at Quarry Woods, by the renowned architectural photographer, Eric de Maré, is situated in a backwater along this stretch.[177] It captures the quirky architectural decoration that earlier boathouse building seemed to inspire. A Tudor-gabled upper structure, heavily decorated with barge-boards, balconies and extensive fenestration provides the first-floor habitation. Below the open recesses of the boathouse are decorated with rustic herringbone patterned, half-cut timbers. This type of work is known as stick architecture, or twig work and is believed to be derived from the Adirondack Hills, USA. It seems natural and whimsical.

Gibraltar Close at Winter Hill is also the dramatic setting for a collection of boathouses which contribute to the story of Thames neo-Tudor. They group neatly into two pairs, and one other, with a more solitary black and white example before the boatyard. Wootten's Boatyard, the hub of the setting, has a half-timbered boathouse, now used as their office headquarters. The land was leased as a boatyard from 1908. The first boathouse, Edgewood, next to the yard, was built around 1908 and has been successfully modernised with an extended balcony; the boathouse beside it has glass insets into the gable and is a contemporary build. The second pair is less restored, with painted timbering and gables. The first of this pair was originally a wet boathouse, now dry, and has a date plaque of 1887. This used to belong to a house called Mayfield, which is now Herries School. Kenneth Grahame, author of *Wind in the Willows*, lived at Mayfield – it is likely that he would have walked down Winter Hill through the 'Wild Wood', below Gibraltar Lane to the boathouse, where he would have heard the wind in the willows and found inspiration for his epic saga of Mole and Ratty. The second of the pair is called Holmwood, believed to have been built around

1890; the owners have heard that the building was used as a lodge for the local Masons. At Holmwood too are the traces in the grass of an old railway track, perhaps used for transporting the chalk. The fifth is a tile-hung boathouse, which a few years ago was rebuilt on a steel frame and restored using the original Victorian tiles, which were made at the tile works at Pinkneys' Green. This was a dry boathouse, but now has a wet dock. The current owners are in possession of a document dated February 1896, leasing the land on which the boathouse stands 'in consideration of the expense incurred by the Lessee in the erection of a boathouse', which means the boathouse predates that date. The use of more environmentally-coloured paints, such as aqua and green which blend with their habitat, alongside glass as an infill material to replace brick or timber, is notable in this collection of boathouses; it seems a sympathetic way to modernise the neo-Tudor. The 1923 Ordnance Survey Map of the area shows a boathouse to the property of Deancroft, one belonging to Waterdale, another dated 1903 and two others, so the numbers seem to add up.

7.30 The White Boathouse
John Clarke 2005

The Thames is a river of contrasts; the stretch after Winter's Hill produces a pristine contemporary boathouse, built in 1988, with accommodation above. Architecturally it makes a play on the Diocletian window; the Maltese cross cut into the glass reflects the history of the previous owner who built it. The property to which it belongs was built on the site of a hunting lodge in the fifteenth century.

7.31 Noah's House Boathouse

The RIBA Photographs Collection *The Architect and Building News* 1932

A little further on are the remains of what is a unique modernist boathouse belonging to Noah's House. It has a flat roof which forms an overhanging hood, and extravagantly curved concrete sides to its external staircase. It is the only Grade II* boathouse on the non-tidal Thames; today it looks unbelievably forlorn, and is desperate for restoration. It was built in 1930 by the builder, Colin Lucas, for his father, as a boathouse and workshop, with a music room above. A contemporary report of the boathouse says that it was designed 'to be used as a bedroom when the bungalow itself [was] full. The boats [were] run up from the river on rollers fixed to the floor, and there [were] ceiling hangers for masts, sails, oars, and boats. The windows which [were] frameless... [ran] the whole length of the building, and the hood over them... [this was] necessary in order to protect the boats from the direct rays of the sun.'

7.32 Plan and Section of Noah's House Boathouse
The RIBA Photographs Collection *The Architect and Building News* 1932

7.33 The Music Room, Noah's House Boathouse
The RIBA Photographs Collection *The Architect and Building News* 1932

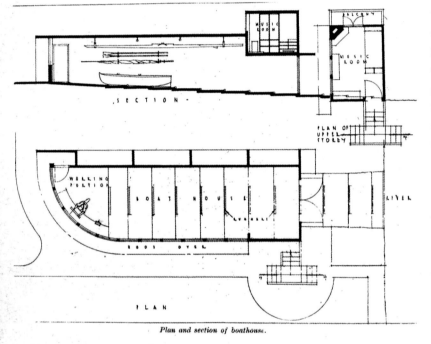

Plan and section of boathouse.

The buildings were erected on a raft as the site often flooded in the winter months. They were 'distempered a medium brown', to integrate into the landscape. The article finishes by suggesting that 'the development of [Colin Lucas'] ideas which can be regarded as valuable research work, will be watched with interest.'[178] The listed building description states that 'Noah's house and its boathouse...were the first reinforced concrete buildings in Britain in the Modern Movement style.'[179] Noah's boathouse is his 'oldest surviving work', showing 'the system of rebating the windows directly into the concrete' which was innovatory at the time, and 'much repeated by architects in the 1950s and 1960s.' The use of concrete as a modern building material was to radically change the face of architecture in Britain; it is extraordinary to think that a small boathouse on the Thames was one of the early prototypes for its use. Lucas went on to build some 'exciting modern houses' in the 1930s with Amyas Connell and Basil Ward.[180]

The plan of Noah's boathouse shows the boathouse space with runners for the boat and a work station with the music room and balcony in the upper storey.

It is a rare to have an internal photograph of living quarters in any early boathouse. The music room of Noah's boathouse is unique as a 1930s room-set, with its rectilinear lines, built in furniture, metal windows looking out over the river, tubular stool, abstract rug and artwork, and Deco-shaped armchair. The arms of the chair interestingly reflect the shape of the boathouse staircase.

7.34 The Upper Thames Sailing Club
John Clarke 2005

There are some great institutional boathouses on the Thames. The Upper Thames Sailing Club, situated on the Spade Oak reach where yachtsmen have traditionally gathered, must be numbered as one of these. It was described in the late nineteenth century by John Leyland, as 'a handsome boathouse'.[181] It shows a central gable, decorated with a rounded timber arch, and the Club's name. A long range of fenestration, balcony (originally with 'X' framing), clap-boarding, an exterior staircase, dry boathouse and a small integral sentinel box, give this building real character and charm. The club held its inaugural meeting at the Ray Mead Hotel, near Boulter's Lock, in October 1884, and moved into their first clubhouse at Townsend's Wharf sometime afterwards. A blossoming membership necessitated them buying a piece of land in early 1890, and erecting a new clubhouse on the site. The architect was a 'Mr Vernon and the builder Mr C.W. Hunt, both of High Wycombe'. It was described at the time as 'a pretty structure situated between the Ferry Hotel...and the old headquarters'. 'There was a club room, [10.5m x 5m], an additional men's room, a bedroom, sail room and balcony. A tennis lawn was promised for a later date, although no more was heard of this scheme; tea on the lawn was a major part of Upper Thames entertainment.'[182] At the far end of the lawn was a small boathouse, more of a large shed, known as the Fury Boathouse; this belonged to a rowing club which had got into financial difficulties, hence its purchase by the club.

At Bourne End too was the Townsend Boatyard founded in 1884, with their boathouses. The boatyard, which was downstream of Shaw's, was sold in 1960s and is now a marina.[183] The 1923 Ordnance Survey Map features three boathouses around Bourne End, one of which would be Shaw and Sons. Shaw also had a yard at Marlow, by the bridge on the town side.

7.35 Barn Boathouse – Cookham
John Clarke 2005

7.36 Cookham neo-Tudor
John Clarke 2005

The neo-Tudor never really deserts the Thames. An Edwardian boathouse on the long approach to Cookham Bridge, with glazed doors and offset square timber framing, has the air of a rather smart Edwardian garage. There is an assortment of boathouses on this stretch, in the area known as the Abbey Estate. Sometimes the simplest has the greatest charm; one rural barn-like example shows a long range of timber with a clay hipped roof with half-circular shapes decorating the front gable. It is believed that this boathouse was built for the steam launch *Pierrette* in 1894. Early-nineteenth-century maps show at least ten boathouses before Cookham Bridge, and two after the bridge. Today this reach is still home to a wide variety of boathouses of varying designs.

Just before Cookham Bridge there is a particularly special wet boathouse, with accommodation over. It is constructed on a brick base with a half-timbered upper floor, and has a gable, balcony, chimney and flagpole and is surrounded by a well-tended garden. It shows the Thames neo-Tudor approaching the Swiss chalet aesthetic. Nearer the bridge, in the 1960s, J.H.B. Peel, described the 'white boathouses on the right bank [these were]...the office of the man who looks after the royal swans.'[184] The Roses' Boathouse was owned by John Turk, a relative of Mike Turk, the current head of the Turk family.

An early 1890's view of Cookham shows the simple commercial boathouses nestling within the boundaries of the iron bridge constructed in 1867. Henry Taunt's entry for Cookham lists Llewellyn's Hotel which advertised the housing of boats.

Cliveden Boathouse stands on a broad, expansive reach of the river, described by Taunt as 'pre-eminently the grandest reach on the Thames'.[185] Somehow, notwithstanding the opulence of the main house, built in the 1860s for the second Duke of Sutherland, one expects something grander. It is a dry boathouse, following traditional boathouse building patterns, having a brick base and half-timbered uppers. 'The steps down to the water were dog-legged with timber to enable boats to be slid over them without damage'.[186] The listed building description writes that 'The west front has [a] Tudor arched boat door with carved spandrels.' Offset gabled wings and eyebrow dormers to the clay roof give some individuality. It

was designed c. 1860 by George Devey (1820-86) – an architect who was to influence pioneers of the Arts and Crafts movement – and is described as a 'picturesque boathouse'.[187] His additions to the fishing-lodge, close-by are infinitely more inspired. The 1923 Ordnance Survey map shows one other boathouse on the Cliveden Reach.

Downstream, at Boulter's Lock, often referred to as the river's Piccadilly, an early photograph shows a simple boathouse, with deep overhanging tiled roof. Jerome K. Jerome set the late-nineteenth-century scene at Boulter's Lock, describing how 'up the stream, and down the stream, [the boats] lie, waiting, their turn, outside the gates, long lines of still more boats...the sunny river...is dotted and decked with yellow, and blue, and orange, and white and red, and pink. All the inhabitants of Hampton and Moulsey [sic] dress themselves up in boating costume, and come and mooch round the lock with their dogs, and flirt, and smoke and watch the boats'.[188] Today Boulter's Lock is still probably one of the busiest locks on the Thames; it is still a 'mooching' point for 'lock-loungers' watching the world go by.[189] The artist G.D. Leslie described how 'Above Boulter's Lock there is a long canalised channel to the mainstream, and by its side...are two boat-houses of picturesque construction, from one of which I painted a picture'.[190]

Maidenhead vies in importance with Henley for its nineteenth-century boathouse architecture. The Boathouse at the Islet c. 1891, on an inlet after the lock, used the neo-Tudor for the boathouse wing, with an upper floor balcony and great barn-like gates. An ornamental bridge and manicured lawns create a harbour of tranquillity for the nineteenth-century boatman. The 1895 *Kelly's Directory* for the area lists Edward Wagg as the owner of The Islet, Maidenhead Court. It is quite possible that Wagg is the man in this picture.

7.38 The Boathouse, The Islet, Maidenhead Court

English Heritage NMR Bedford Lemere 1891

7.39 The Dining Room, The Islet, Maidenhead Court

English Heritage NMR Bedford Lemere 1889

7.40 The Bedroom, The Islet Boathouse, Maidenhead Court

English Heritage NMR Bedford Lemere 1891

An 1891 photograph of Hanbury's Boathouse, also at Maidenhead, shows the neo-Tudor, coupled with the looks of a Swiss chalet.[191] Stout pillars surround a robust ground floor of brick construction, creating a loggia of Gothic arches; the first floor balcony extends round the whole building.

In the late nineteenth century Maidenhead competed with Henley as 'the' place to boat; the elite Guards Boat Club had its headquarters near the bridge, and held their annual regatta in the town. Not surprisingly Ordnance Survey maps of Maidenhead show a proliferation of boathouses, both private and commercial.[192] The 1932 map shows the Boat House of the Islet, off the Thames on a small tributary called White Brooke. Further substantial homes on this reach, such as Riverside, nearby the Islet, had boathouses. In between the properties of The Court and Weir House, was the Maidenhead Boating Company, which provided 'electric canoes and motor launches' for hire. The earlier 1899 Ordnance Survey map shows five boathouses on the river, with three dry boathouses belonging to the substantial properties of Intheray, Somersham and Wynford, set back from the river. The 1923 edition shows Maidenhead Court, Somerlea, and Weir House as having boathouses. Intriguingly the architectural photographer Bedford Lemere's albums, held by the National Record Office, has pictures of three houses, described as Wilkinson's Boathouse, Dr Lissas' Boathouse and Boxall's Boathouse; the photographs however do not show the actual boathouses. The 1899 *Kelly's Directory* for the area does however list all three boathouses at Maidenhead Court.[193] Lieutenant-Colonel Charles Boxall lived at Battlemead, Samuel De Lissa at the Court and Henry Wilkinson was resident at the Weir House.

Approaching Maidenhead Bridge the black and white tower boathouse is a memorable landmark. With a 1930s-style wet boathouse to its side, the square tower shows half-timbering, a balcony, an ornate cornice and a leaded pyramid-shaped roof, topped by a weather-vane. It is one of the river's eye-catchers. Its original use was as a water-tower; barges would moor up alongside to replenish their stocks from an ornate tap which the present owner remembers. It is believed that the foundations to the boathouse are of greenheart, one of the strongest woods in existence. Greenheart was commonly used for 'warehouse floors, piles, jetties and engine fittings'.[194]

Over a century before an 1880s photograph shows a timbered, rustic boathouse, with a distinctive louvred spire and dormers, in the same vicinity. This no longer exists. Henry Taunt mentioned the Boat Houses of J. Bond at Maidenhead Bridge; a rather faded picture of these is held by the Maidenhead Library. The artist G.D. Leslie, who was interested in boathouses, having built one himself at Wallingford, describes 'a pretty little boat-house by the side of the eyot', which could have been this one.[195]

7.42 The Timber and Tin Boatshed
John Clarke 2005

Immediately after the bridge is a tin boatshed, still in commercial use. The building has timber uprights for its frame, but is infilled with corrugated iron. The effect, softened by age and colour, seems very pleasing.

Henry Taunt's entry for Maidenhead describes how the 'riverside at Ray Mead, along to Maidenhead Bridge, has grown very fashionable within the last few years...dotted with villa residences, and two good hotels stand on the bank'.[196] When new housing came to the river, the modern adjunct of a boathouse was not far behind. The Maidenhead Rowing Club had its boathouse close by the bridge, until it moved across the river into its new headquarters in 1998, a three-bay modern neo-Tudor building.[197]

Soon after on the opposite bank of the river there is an elongated, gabled and heavily-glazed boathouse with a pyramid-shaped clay-tiled roof, peering from its ivy shield, with a rather spooky air. It is tall and thin and has the appearance of a sentinel box. The boathouse was purchased by the present owners in 1988, having been derelict for some time. It could have been attached to the hotel close by, or to a private house.

7.44 The Green Mesh Boathouse
John Clarke 2005

7.45 The Contemporary Spire Boathouse
John Clarke 2005

The river flows on towards Bray, past a 'tent' boathouse and onto a pair of contemporary buildings in The Fisheries, the first having a painted mesh steel water-gate and decorative fretwork, with a circular eyelet in the pediment, deep eaves and a tiled roof. It is a fresh approach using a simple gable, but inserting contemporary steelwork to create a decorative, somewhat Japanese-like effect. It was built in 2000 by a landscape gardener, Anthony Paul of Surrey. The second has a rectangular brick entrance; its upper section looks to the past in its heavily-glazed balcony area, and is topped by a rather strange, but purposeful, glazed spire on the clay-tiled roof. Both are wet boathouses.

Further on there is a white boathouse, whose balustrade gives it a Regency air. Close by is the culinary village of Bray, where chefs in chequered trousers are a common sight in the street. At Bray Lock Taunt reminds us that H. Woodhouse had premises advertising 'Boats to be let and housed'.[198] Monkey Island separates this from a dark blue-and-tan timbered boathouse of contemporary and sturdy construction, c. 1998, belonging to the wildly Gothic Oakley Court Hotel. The house was earlier known as Water Oakley, and had belonged to Lord Otto Fitzgerald. It is an unusual design for a modern boathouse, in that the accommodation and separate wet boathouse are joined by an intersecting wing. Although built in the last decade, it has traditional timber-framing. It must be one of the few Thames boathouses with conference facilities and air-conditioning.

7.46 The Oakley Court Boathouse
John Clarke 2005

There follows a long stretch which is devoid of boathouses. The 1932 Ordnance Survey Map shows the Eton boathouses and two others close by Windsor Bridge. A contemporary view of the Eton boathouses, or 'Rafts' as the area is known, shows how boating at the school increased by the late nineteenth century. Today the school's boating regime has changed again; boys now mainly boat from a state-of-the-art rowing lake and clubhouse at Dorney. The boatsheds on the Thames are used for storing boats and boat restoration, and the area feels unused.

The Eton Boating Book 1816-32 describes how historically 'little is known of the early days of Eton rowing, and still less of the boathouses from which Wetbobs [rowers] obtained their boats. Until 1840 boys were not officially allowed on the river, and on several occasions those caught were flogged'.[199] A picture of Wyndesor [sic] Bridge dated 1763 shows 'only two buildings...on the Eton side, one of which was 'possibly...the boathouse of the Pipers [brothers]'. The poet Shelley was in the sixth form in 1810. An Eton beak (master) William Cory, wrote about his early life, describing how Shelley 'would plunge down Brocas Lane, past a hot den where clay pipes were made, dodge the curved beaks of boats under repair...scamper down a rickety staircase on a single plank that ran out into the river...[and] jump into his boat'.[200] By 1829 the 'two boathouses of Tolladays and Hesters' are mentioned, and by 1840 the 'boathouses begin to take more definite shape', with Searles and Salters setting up boathouses in the area. G.F. Winter, the Cambridge boat builder, took a property in 1885 and provided 'superior management and the provision of better boats'. It is evident from these accounts that Eton's early boating relied on the independent boat builders for their provision of boats. In 1888 it was suggested that 'the school ought to have its own boathouse and its own boats'. The Brocas Boat House Company was formed and 'a good deal was also spent on a new boathouse'. Improvements were made in the 1900s, and in 1923 a large addition of [6m x 21.5m] was made to

the boathouse, with the removal of the Old VIII Room from the ground to the upper floor. An 1834 plan of the boathouse area shows Winter's Boatyard, a tin-shed, 'Pilkington' boathouse, 'Froggie's' boathouse, the 'Yard', and the 'Eight Raft', the latter being the upstream end.[201] Today Rafts appears to be made up of five main buildings: a large modern block with first floor balconies and flats above with three boathouse bays below, a three-gabled neo-Tudor building, a red brick two bay round-arched boathouse, a further gabled nineteenth-century building, with another range and a lean-to at the upstream end. One senses development is in the air.

The Eton College Rowing Lake boathouse at Dorney was designed by Herbert J. Stribling and Partners in 2000, and opened by Kate Hoey as Minister for Sports and the Arts. Function supersedes aesthetics; the centre is a highly successful location for regattas and rowing championships. It is designated as the venue for rowing and flat-water canoeing for the 2012 Olympics.

After Windsor the 1932 Ordnance Survey maps show two boathouses in the Datchet area and one by Old Windsor Lock. *Salter's Guide* of 1913 lists The King's Boathouse in the Home Park, after the Victoria Bridge, and opposite Datchet. On the Salter's map it is marked as the Royal Boat House.[202] Jane Roberts' history of the Park describes how 'in 1861 work was completed on a brick and timber residence on the towpath at the eastern end of the Broadwater stream: it was named Albert

Cottage and was built to Teulon's designs. A boat house adjoined the cottage; it was built to house the Royal Barge, which was still used on the River Thames.'[203] The boathouse is not open to the public, but the listed building entry describes the cottage and the boathouse: 'red brick, instepped weathered 1st floor, timber-framed gabled projection. Date plaque with crown and cipher. Gable brick boathouse on edge of pool linked to cottage by pierced balustrade which is returned over cut to river'.[204] Samuel Sanders Teulon (1812-73) was a Gothic Revival architect renowned for his 'startlingly original' churches and other buildings.[205] The archives at Windsor Castle have a colour-washed drawing of the Home Park Boathouse, with plan, which shows a brick and timber building, with gables and braced timbers. The entrance shows a decorative barge-board with ornamental bosses. It is dated 1861.

From Windsor there is another great stretch of river devoid of boathouses, making rather dull viewing for any boathouse hunter. At the Bell Weir Lock, near Egham, only Taunt's 1870s entry reminds us that there were 'Boats to let, housed or taken care of' at The Anglers' Rest Inn. Further downstream at Staines Bridge the Swan Hotel had a boathouse, as did the Chertsey Bridge Hotel.[206] At Staines too were Tims' boathouses, and further on at Laleham was the famous Harris' Boatyard.[207]

At Shepperton George Purdue had a working boatshed near Ferry Square.[208] The first contemporary boathouse of interest on this stretch was, until recently, on Shepperton Lock Island. The Weybridge Mariners had their club and boathouse there; this was unfortunately destroyed by fire in March 2006. The history of the club and boathouse is interesting. In 1972 The Thames Conservancy offered the club a years' lease in order to convert a nineteenth-century barge repair workshop, on the island, into a club and boathouse. The workshop had fallen into disrepair. One of the club's members was a civil engineer and he and other members re-built the building, keeping the original profile. They now face the more daunting task of starting from scratch again, after the fire completely gutted the building.

8.1 The Old Thames Conservancy Barge Repair Shop
Weybridge Mariners c. 1970s

Onwards from Shepperton and after Walton Bridge, next door to the Angler's Hotel, is the Thameside Boathouse Terrace, a red brick Victorian range, with covered first-floor balconies, and four boathouse bays below. In the nineteenth century the public house, The Swan, was next door. Clark's boatyard with boathouses stood beside the Swan and the Rosewell boatyard, with its boathouses further upstream, 'between the backwater and the bridge'. The local historian, Brian Ellis, writes that both [boatyards] hired out boats, gave navigational instruction and also swimming lessons.[209] The picture, from the Frith Collection, shows the Swan Hotel, the Boathouse Terrace and the Anglers pub beyond in 1908. It is interesting to note that in 1850 there were eight boat-builders on the Thames from Chertsey to Richmond; by 1900, with the rise in popularity of boating, this number had risen to forty-four. The number today is probably nearer the 1850 figure.[210]

Just downstream from Sunbury Lock stands the most endearing clap-board sentinel-box boathouse, known as Riverbank Boathouse. Standing high on the bank, with a steep dry ascent to its wooden doors, it has a balcony on three sides, French windows and a clay-tiled roof, with a terracotta dragon guarding its territory. Its owners, one of whom is an architect, have a wealth of information on the boathouse, which is now along with the house, Grade II listed.[211] The house was in a horrendously dilapidated state in the late 1970s when they decided to make an offer. They bought the house 'in its grotty falling-down state because of the garden and in particular [because of] the quality of the boathouse'. With little money to spare, and even though they did not at the time own the boathouse in entirety – ownership is shared with the Environment Agency – they spent every penny they could to get it stabilised, strengthening the frame and re-cladding much of the building. The balcony was at that time supported on some rather ugly stained posts; it was decided that the balcony should be self-supporting. During these renovations 'we found that two workmen put their names on the back of the internal boarding, which, if my memory serves me correctly, said October 1888. I think their names were Bob and John. It seems to me that it is fairly consistent in style with building of that time, e.g. the Bridgenorth tiles were certainly being made in that period, and the first floor room's interior wood boarding is totally consistent with the late 1880-90s.' Early Ordnance Survey maps shows that the building 'was originally built as a gazebo in the middle of the garden, that existed before the Thames Conservancy doubled the width of the river on this reach...so that by the time the river was widened the gazebo ended up on the riverbank. I presume that at that time the slipway was made and the building altered to allow boats to be drawn up to or possibly into the building.' The original weathervane and terracotta dragon, with demountable wings, were unfortunately stolen from the building in the last three years, but have since been replaced. The dragon was specially cast by a Welsh potter. The boathouse is really a delight and remains a landmark both for river-users and walkers, including the girls from Lady Eleanor Holles School and the boys from Hampton School and Molesey Boat Club, all of whom treat it as a marker for the end of their training runs. The boathouse 'has [also] played a significant role in supporting the Sunbury Millennium Embroidery Project, allowing us to store a great many artefacts associated with this project'. The ground floor of the boathouse was also used as a small theatre, where a local group put on 'Twelfth Night, reviews and other theatrical extravaganzas'.

So we have a gazebo, built by Bob and John c. 1888, which became a boathouse only by virtue of the Thames being widened, and which has ultimately served as a family boathouse for nearly thirty years, hosting thespian gatherings and a Millennium project. It is currently undergoing further restoration.

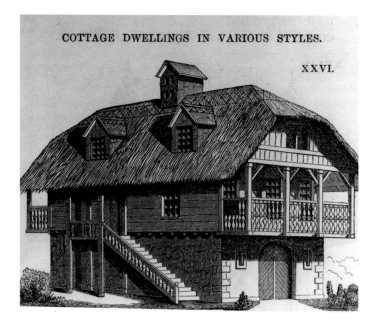

COTTAGE DWELLINGS IN VARIOUS STYLES.

XXVI.

8.4 A Cottage Dwelling in the German Swiss Style
The Encyclopaedia of Cottage, Farm Villa Architecture and Furniture (1833, 2000)
RIBA Photographs Collection

Further on past Garrick's Eyot and the Astoria (the 1913 houseboat , used by Fred Karno, the Edwardian music hall owner, who housed a full orchestra on its upper deck) we come to what is one of the most extraordinary and extravagant boathouses on the Thames, close to Tagg's Island. The Grade II listed, three-storey building, with extensive balconies, is an original Swiss chalet; one more layer however and it would be a Chinese pagoda. It has long ranges of fenestration, intricately-carved fretwork to the barge-boards, and three tiers of ornately panelled balconies, achieving a somewhat wild union. Two sturdy staircases and the sheer size of the building suggest it might well have originally been conceived as a club.[212] This is a balcony house, one to view and be viewed from. In 2005 the boathouse was looking a little forlorn and had just been sold. No doubt it will be restored. Even in a rather uncared for state it represents an extravaganza of boathouse architecture.

The earliest known photograph of the building is by Bedford Lemere, and is dated around 1888. Apparently it was shipped in prefabricated form from Switzerland, and transported up river in barges c. 1882 for the garden of a house called Riverholm, which was demolished in the 1920s. Swiss chalets were not uncommon, Charles Dickens apparently built one, and it is believed there was a large one in the grounds of Danesfield House, at Medmenham on the Thames. In 1833 John Loudon published his *Encyclopaedia of Cottage, Farm and Villa Architecture*, which provided a design compendium of mass-housing, aimed at the

landowner keen on modern developments. He featured the Swiss chalet as a design type for cottage dwellings. Wooden construction, deep eaves, a balcony, turned railings, sash windows, external staircases and large decorated brackets were dominant design features, most of which are found in English nineteenth-century boathouses.

A previous owner of the Hucks' Boatyard Swiss chalet writes that 'It was initially used as a boathouse by its owner Mr O'Hagan, who was 'purported to have won the freehold from Edward VII on the spin of a roulette wheel at the property.' By the late 1900s the building was known as O'Hagan's Boathouse. The boathouse was purchased just after World War I by Mr Frank Hucks, a naval architect, who developed it as a boatyard. Around 1932 'a deal was struck with the Thames Conservators', land was exchanged and the present format of the wharf was created, with the weir downstream. After her husband's death Mrs Hucks opened a restaurant with hotel facilities on the first floor, which she ran until the late 1930s. In the summer tables were laid out in the garden. After World War II, her son Richard Hucks took over the running of the boatyard, which became a successful business. He later built a slipway and dry dock. Tragically he fell to his death in the dry dock in March 1996. Mrs Hucks then ran the business down, and deregulated the property to residential use, until her death in 2003. Close to the Swiss cottage were the famous Thorneycroft Boatyards at Platt's Eyot, with their commercial boathouses, Garrick's Villa and the Waterworks.

8.5 Hucks' Boathouse

English Heritage NMR Bedford Lemere 1888

8.6 Tagg's New Boating Premises

RIBA Photographs Collection *The Building News* April 11th 1890

New Boating Premises for T G Tagg + Son at East Molesey

A Burnell Burnell Architect New Stone Buildings 59 Chancery Lane WC

Opposite Tagg's Island was the boatyard of Messrs. Tom Tagg and Son, boat and steam launch builders. *The Building News* of April 11th 1890 shows a drawing for their new boathouse, which was an addition to their already extensive premises. The ground floor had a large storage area for boats, 9m x 24.5m 'so that the longest boat can be easily moved'. 'The floor is of asphalte, with railway metal bedded in to run the boats on. Lavatories and dressing-rooms are provided on this floor, and the grounds laid out for lawn-tennis, gardens, and stables. The upper floors are arranged for club premises, ladies' dressing-room...and show-rooms'. The building was rough cast, with two gables and a veranda to the central section, tall chimneys, half-timbering and a generous balcony wrapping the front and sides. The architect was Mr Burnell-Burnell, of Chancery Lane, London WC.[213]

Further down past Hampton Court the river takes its great meander and runs on down to Kingston Bridge. Just past the bend, before Kingston Bridge, Taunt writes that the Raven Ait Boat Company had boats to 'let and housed'.[214] On the Teddington side, after the railway bridge, is a building which is now land-locked, but would appear to have been a boathouse. This is a Ruskinian multi-coloured buff and red brick Victorian delight.[215] It has an emphasised arched entrance with modern glazed doors, and a heavily-articulated barge-board, painted a Gitane blue. A centrally placed oeil-de-boeuf is placed to its apex. Its design has the aesthetics of a Victorian pumping station.

8.8 The Cream Swiss Chalet
John Clarke 2005

The river seems to take on a new persona around Teddington; black swans with vivid red beaks circle, and canoeists follow the wash of power-boats like predators in the sea.

The Teddington Reach is power-dressed with boathouses. One of the most memorable is the cream Swiss chalet, c. 1840s, half-timbered, on a brick base with pebble dash infill, whose twisted baluster balcony is supported by gigantic paired brackets. It is broad and generous with wide-slatted water-gates, expansive fenestration and three-sided decks, with a rear staircase. It was built as the boathouse to the Broom Park Estate and has a wet dock and oblong room above. Leyland features a photograph of it in his late 1890's publication of the Thames. At one point it was used as an ironing room for the big house. Its design is luxurious and assured, emulating both the Arts and Crafts and the Swiss cottage aesthetic.

Another fine boathouse follows. Built of red brick, as a dry boathouse, it has a generous trellised balcony, providing decks on all three sides, with a half-timbered gable, painted cream with white timberwork. The side elevation shows a simple tablet of pargetting, a patterned plaster-work, set in between the brick and pebbledash.[216] The front gable is heavily decorated with a barge-board, showing foliate bosses set in square relief. A full width of glazing, with some coloured top-lights, decorates the upper façade, with opening top-lights for ventilation. To the ground floor the iron pillars supporting the balcony have decorative brackets. It is another luxurious example of its type. The 1894 Ordnance Survey map shows ten boathouses on the Teddington bank from Richmond Bridge to Tathim's Island (now Steven's Eyot), some belonging to substantial properties such as Weir Bank, Moiravale, Chesfield, and further on to Old Broom Hall and Broom Hall, where the maps show at least six more boathouses leading up to the lock.[217]

Turk's boathouse has long been a feature of the Thames at Kingston; Henry Taunt describes him as a 'Boat Punt and Canoe Builder'.[218] Mike Turk, the present owner, who took over from his father in 1956, tells how the boatyard was established around 1710 at Kingston. The original premises were at a barge house on the Down Hall Estate; these were later extended with a variety of boats, punts, and rowing boats being built in the boathouse. Turk's exhibited at the Great Exhibition of 1851 and exported world-wide, notably to the Himalayas, Bombay and New Queensland. By 1895 the demand was such that the Albany Boathouse was commissioned on the Teddington Reach. A drawing of the frontal elevation, dated 1968, shows a sturdy two-storey brick built building, with boathouse area, balconies and extensive fenestration. Boats were constructed on the top floor, using trap doors to lower them to the varnishing areas below. Kingston Rowing Club, Tiffin's School, and Kingston Grammar and the Royal Canoe Club all shared the boathouse facilities with Turk's. The site was sold around twenty years ago and the business moved to the historic dockyards at Chatham. A small floating office is maintained at Kingston.

Individuality is the hallmark of this reach. The Royal Canoe Club's clap-board façade on Trowlock Island, shows a low, wide pediment within which is displayed its royal insignia, complete with crossed paddles, and the dates 1866-1897. The club's boatsheds are positioned symmetrically to either side of the balcony in a lean-to fashion, with sliding blue doors. The club was inaugurated in 1866, and was established on the island in the following year, with the boathouse being built in 1897, to the designs of a member, C. H. Cooper, the Borough Surveyor for Wimbledon. It is believed that the lean-to additions were probably a little later. The club originally held the land as tenants until 1931, when they purchased the freehold. Plans were underway in 2005 to replace the old clubhouse with a new timber-framed building, whose substructure will be sheet-piled. Flooding has always been a problem; the existing floors have been raised a few times, so much so that the internal dados in the old building are half-way up the walls. The design of the new building reflects the old, and will show the Club badge on its façade. A member, who is familiar with Rangoon in Burma, notes that there are many similar buildings on the riverbank there.

8.10 The Brookdale Boathouse
Kim Wilkie 1992

Nearing the end of our journey opposite Teddington Lock, at the start of the tidal Thames, there is a splendidly rakish wooden boathouse, with its brick side walls high above the water, showing a steep ascent to its gates. The first floor has a projecting balcony, French windows and an open timbered gable, decorated with a wooden finial. A long first floor clerestory runs behind, with the wet boathouse accommodation below.

The re-named Aldous Boathouse (earlier sometimes known as the Wet Boathouse) was a Victorian wet and dry boathouse, built in 1870 to reflect the architecture of its villa, Brookdale, on Manor Road, Teddington. The house has since been demolished and replaced by a block of flats. Brookdale, like many of its riverside neighbours, had a summer-house with wet and dry boathouse facilities, and a large garden.[219] Such boathouses are traditionally the most suitable way to store wooden boats, which, whilst ideally needing constant moisture, do not need immersion 24/7. Early photographs show the boathouse with a pair of derricks which were used to lift the boat for land storage; the summerhouse section sits above. In addition to this riverside viewing area Brookdale had a 'widow's walk' on the roof; this flat structure with iron grilles on the apex of the roof allowed extensive views of the river, and was also apparently known to be a useful place for young people of the time to 'lose' their chaperones.

8.11 The Aldous Boathouse, Teddington

Sam S. Levy 2008

With Brookdale demolished the developers, St George, put in planning application for a new development. Unfortunately during the building process, in 1998, the boathouse was burnt down. The following year Sylvia Wicks, a jewellery designer, who was brought up on the water in Newport, Australia, bought a 999 year lease on the charred remains, and took on the daunting responsibility of re-building it. The fire damaged bricks were reused in the rebuilding process. With the help of their architect, Nicholas Norden of Neale and Nordon, they located the perfect brick match, only to find later that they had inadvertently gone to a brickyard just two miles from the original supplier. Oak framing, traditionally marked, and cedar cladding were selected to ensure a building which would last, the design very much reflecting the original, except for the dry boathouse to the rear. The piece of land to the side of the boathouse has been treated with as much care as the boathouse. With help from the Environment Agency it was determined that this should be planted to reflect the riverside habitat, encouraging the growth of wild plants, many of which live naturally along the riverside. Today there are over sixty individual species on the site, including chickweed, comfrey, mallow, hemlock and wild carrot. The boathouse is well known to many on the river; Keith and Sylvia Wicks encourage the Sea Cadets and other friends to use it. It features briefly in the film *Dunkirk*; it stands adjacent to the original site of Tough's boatyard, where many of the little ships left for their historic voyage to Dunkirk in 1940.

This mid-twentieth century photograph shows Tough's boatyard at Teddington which was adjacent to the Aldous Boathouse. This is a commercial boathouse of one gable with shallow-arched boat bays below, barn doors and lean-to additions.

Both Taunt and Leyland mention another boathouse, which was situated on this reach: the Chinese-Gothic house, built on the site of Pope's villa c. 1878 had a similarly styled boathouse. It had trellis-work gates and an overhanging viewing area with 'X' framed balustrading. The house was built by Thomas Young, a tea merchant who bought the site in 1842. It later became St Catherine's Convent School. The original Palladian home of Alexander Pope was destroyed at the beginning of the nineteenth century by its owner, Lady Howe, who was thereafter known as the 'Queen of the Goths'.[220]

8.12 Tough's Teddington Boathouse

English Heritage NMR c. 1945-65

8.13 Teddington Boathouse

John Clarke 2005

The river takes us on down to Richmond, past a boathouse that is probably unknown to most. Its entrance is covered in ivy, but shows important stone brackets to either side of the arch; if you take a skiff and row in you enter a cavernous brick vault with birds nesting on the blocked-up round windows, which form the upper part of the building. The remains of an internal iron staircase show that this was, at one point, a building of quality. The deep-water boathouse stands adjacent to a block of modern flats and seems totally unused. Some would say that its charm is that it should remain so.[221]

The 'Tarpaulin Man' is another interesting feature of this stretch of the river, who lives on a raft under an evolving structure of corrugated iron and tarpaulins, with a solar panel and water garden growing beside him, overlooked by the unforgettable mass of Sir Edwin Cooper's Star and Garter Home (1921-4), high on Richmond Hill. A pair of sturdy brick built Romanesque arched boathouses, with stone keystones, stand quite close to each other on this last stretch, before the tidal Thames proper. After Teddington there is one more lock at Richmond, which is half tidal, before the river is open to the sea.

The first of this pair has a stone-faced arch for its water entrance, timber and pebble-dash accommodation above, with a sturdy balcony, French windows and a hipped tiled roof. The second has a wider brick platform with a similar water-arch, with stone keystones set into the brick and an iron water-gate. Small brick piers break the balustrading, and protect a black and white timbered and gabled pavilion, with a hipped clay-tiled roof. The current owner has no knowledge of its building date, but believes it was built prior to the lock at Richmond.

The river changes dramatically from Lechlade to Teddington; the quieter market towns of the upper reaches merge into the more cosmopolitan Henley and meander on through some resplendent scenery. Slowly it opens out into the wider, more suburban habitat of Hampton Court, with its extraordinary mix of the grand and the bungalow, before finally reaching Teddington. Private boathouses far outnumber the commercial and the institutional.[222] Surprisingly there seems to be both distinguished and simple boathouses on most stretches; the nature of the reach, whether rural or urban, does not necessarily seem to dictate the nature of the boathouse. The democracy of the river has always been one of its greatest charms.

Boathouse design around the world embraces the universal and the national. It seems particularly interesting that every type of boathouse form worldwide – the timbered gable and balcony, the boathouse terrace, the 'A' frame, the Swiss chalet, the barn and the hut on water – are found together on one river in England, the non-tidal Thames. In Britain the Thames reveals an extravagant variety of boathouse architecture. Historically the British, with their love of the idiosyncratic, seem to have the edge on some of the world's distinctive boathouses. Ballrooms mix with Swiss cottages, plunge pools with fishing temples, miniature castles with crouching dragons and thatched boathouses. The sheer classical elegance of the Fishing Temple at Kedleston shares its place in boathouse history with the unique roofline of the Dougarie boathouse on the shores of Arran in the western isles of Scotland. Artists, poets and writers are drawn to the water. Agatha Christie's double tenure of the Wallingford clap-board and the more illustrious Greenway boathouse on the Dart is perhaps unique. The poet Dylan Thomas' need for Laugharne is undisputed. On the Thames the wild extravaganza of the Tagg's Island Swiss chalet mixes with the modernist lines of the 1930s Noah's boathouse.

Contemporary architects such as Terry Farrell and Shahriar Nassar have produced boathouses that can be judged equal to many of our new iconic, land-lubbed buildings. Boathouse design is enjoying a revival, with innovative use of material and form. PLOT's rolling decks in Copenhagen, Turner Brooks' nautical boathouse in the USA, the leaning port control tower at Lisbon and Shahriar Nasser's copper-bladed roof at Oxford are visually very exciting. Newly built are Sarah Wigglesworth Architects' two Corten steel-clad boxes at the Cremorne Riverside Centre, near London's Battersea Bridge. These 'rusting' boxes, one an office, the other a boat shelter, show sharp industrial edges, punctured by what appear to be' bullet' holes. They are a dramatic reference to the container-land environment of the disused power station and recycling plants in which they stand, and show, that as a country with a history of inspired boathouse design, we are widening our perspective yet again.[223]

There is very little boathouse building on the Thames today compared to the late-nineteenth-century period; planning restraints in the flood plain make the likelihood of a renaissance highly improbable. It is still noticeable how many modern boathouses reflect our native fascination with the neo-Tudor. It remains a style which is deeply symbolic of our land, and our national identity. However, some brave modernists are prepared to seek planning for the inspirational glass box, which integrates easily with water and foliage. The Thames environment and habitat are little changed; technology and its machinery have hardly touched its course. It remains a place, in common with many waterside habitats, where it is possible to escape the pressures of life, and lose oneself in another world. Alan De Botton writes that 'what we lack in society we try to achieve in architecture'.[224] Certainly, in boathouse terms, it seems that this is true the world over.

Footnotes

Introduction

1 De Botton, A. (2006) pp. 188 & 205.
The Architecture of Happiness: London.

Chapter 1 : Boathouses Around the World

2 PLOT has since disbanded. The two former partners
have started two new companies JDS Architects and
BIG Bjarke Ingels Group. The two partners are
supervising the completion of the Ellsinore
Psychiatric Hospital, the Sjakket HQ in Copenhagen as
well as a handful of designs for objects, lamps and
typefaces.
3 *Icon*, Nos. 14-18, July-December 2004, pp. 32-33.
'The [sailing] school and [youth] club occupy opposite
corners of the square site; the school is housed in an
L-shaped building on the waterfront and the boatstore
in a wedge-shaped space that rises to a point to
provide storage for tall items such as masts'.
The interior picture shows a multi-purpose room.
4 The translation for the name is 'no man is a prophet
in their own land' - Aalto named his boat 'when he
was receiving more acclaim abroad than in Finland',
Building Design, July 30th 1999, p. 5.
5 Schildt, Göran, (2007) p. 629, *Alvar Aalto - His Life*.
This statement was taken from a eulogy Aalto
delivered for the architect Eliel Saarinen in 1950.
6 This information is translated from various sources
in Germany.
7 *Kippo News*, June 2005. Ministry Education, Culture,
Sports and Technology, Tokyo, Japan.
8 *Voyage de la Corvette l'Astrolabe* (1830-35) Paris: J.
Tastu. The National Library of Australia. Rex Nan
Kivell Collection. The drawings are by Louis de
Sainson. Louis Leborne copied the drawing of the
boat hangar by de Sainson, and reproduced it as a
lithograph. Leborne was head of the drawing school in
Nancy, France.
9 The Boldt Castle Yacht House, Thousand Islands.
10 For a magnificent collection of Canadian
boathouses see De Visser, J. and Ross, J. (2006)
Boathouses.
11 Ibid. p. 71.
12 Yale University - Official Athletic Site, Gilder
Boathouse and Turner Brooks Architects.
13 *Arkkitehti* 2, 2002 pp. 60-65.

Chapter 2 : The British Boathouse

14 The National Trust - Greenway Boathouse. 2007.
15 Christie, A. (1956, 2005 edition) p.509, *Poirot The
Complete Ariadne Oliver - Dead Man's Folly*.
16 The Dylan Thomas Boathouse at Laugharne -
Carmarthenshire County Council.
17 Thomas, D. Letter to Princess Caetani, 1952.
Carmarthenshire County Council - The Dylan Thomas
Boathouse at Laugharne.
18 A saddle is a ridge connecting two higher
elevations of a roof.

19 *Country Life*, August 8th 1996, pp. 37-40.
20 *Country Life* 1st August 1996 and 8th August 1996.
21 Stuart Gray, A. (1985) pp. 181-183, *Edwardian
Architecture*. Flockhart was a Scottish architect who
studied at the Glasgow School of Art and later formed
his own successful practice in London. He designed
the premises for Duveen Brothers, the art dealers in
Bond Street, 120 Long Acre, The Hall, Parkwood,
Henley-on-Thames, nos. 11 and 13 Landsowne Road
and the Royal State Rooms on SS *Balmoral Castle* for
the Union Castle Line amongst others. Mills, J.
Hesling, H. Maclean, M. and K. (1996) *Rosehaugh -
A House of Its Time*.
22 A crenellation is found on the parapet of a building
and is formed with alternating higher and lower
sections. The National Trust - Fell Foot Park and
English Heritage Listed Building Descriptions: 421910,
421911, 421912 & 421913.
23 *The Architect's Journal*, no. 200, 18 August 1994,
July - December 1994, pp. 16-17.
24 Curl. J. (1999) p. 79, *Oxford Dictionary of
Architecture*.
25 Mott, G. and Sample Aall, S. (1989) pp. 78-79,
Follies and Pleasure Pavilions.
26 Roberts, J. (1997) *Royal Landscape - The Gardens
and Parks of Windsor*.
27 Ibid p. 356.
28 Ibid. p. 429.
29 Ibid. p. 357.
30 Curl. J.S. Op.cit. p. 698.
31 Roberts, J. Op.cit. p. 417.
32 Ibid p. 431.
33 Ibid. p. 433.

Chapter 3 : Thames Boathouses

34 The non-tidal Thames runs from Lechlade, close to
its source, down to Teddington. The ensuing reach
down to Richmond, with its half-tidal lock, is an area
with some important boathouse building, and was
therefore included in the study. Just beyond
Richmond, at Syon House, was an important classical
boathouse designed by Robert Mylne (1733-1811) for
the Duke of Northumberland. This was pulled down
when the Thames was embanked in the area, but its
pavilion still stands, and is in use today.
Architectural styles:
The Arts and Crafts movement was popularised by
the artist and craftsman William Morris (1834-96) and
by architects such as Philip Webb (1831-1915) and
William Lethaby (1857-1931). It was a movement
inspired by honesty to materials and craftsmanship,
paying homage to the medieval guilds, opposing the
rise of the machine and of manufacturing.
The Queen Anne style was popular from the 1860s; its
distinctive features were red brickwork, rubbed-brick
arches, elongated white sash windows, bay windows,
emphasised chimneys, steep pitched roofs, balconies
and terracotta work. See Curl, J.S. Op.cit.
The Elizabethan Renaissance became fashionable as a
stylistic trend in the 1890s, when architects were

seeking to re-create and emphasise England's
architectural heritage. Our native Elizabethan
architecture, which they were seeking to emulate, was
noted for its distinctive high pitched gables, bay
windows, emphasised door-cases and ornate
brickwork.
The Edwardian Baroque is a term used to describe
architecture of the 1900s which sought a revival of
our national styles; it made reference to the Baroque
architecture of Wren (1632-1723) Hawksmoor (1661-
1736) and Vanbrugh (1664-1726), seeking to emulate
and over-emphasise classical features in a way the
more serious Baroque would never have envisaged.
The concept of nationalism was being celebrated in
this neo-revival; Wren, Hawksmoor and Vanbrugh
were all native-born Englishmen.
35 This includes Sherriff's Boathouse at the
Redgrave-Pinsent Rowing Lake at Caversham, which
is adjacent to the river.
36 Belloc, H. (1907, 1988) pp. 8-9, *The Historic
Thames*. Belloc writes that the Thames is 'only 215
miles from source to mouth' nothing compared to the
'titanic scale' of the Amazon, Mississippi, and Yangtze
Kiang. The word Thames, he claims, is probably
derived from the Sanskrit 'tamasa', meaning dark
water or dark river. Tamesis is a Latin version of the
Celtic word'; earlier spellings are Tames, or Themmes,
but by the 1600s Thames is believed to have become
'the standard spelling'.
37 Peel, J.H.B. (1967) pp. 29-30, *Portrait of the
Thames from Teddington to the Source. Salter's Guide
to the Thames* (1914) p. 13. The guide notes that 'in
1886 the Thames Navigation Act placed the whole
river, upper and lower, under one body, the Thames
Conservancy...it was not until 1908 that the upper
river was again given separate management. Under
the Port of London Act of that year, a re-constituted
Thames Conservancy now has control of the non-tidal
river above Teddington, while the Port of London
Authority is responsible for all below.' Thacker, F.
(1914, 1968), p. 252, *The Thames Highway*. Thacker is
the ultimate authority on the history of the Thames;
he writes that the Thames Preservation Act 1885 'was
the first Act specifically directed towards the
"preservation of the River above Teddington lock for
purposes of public recreation, and for regulating the
pleasure traffic therein."
38 Many think of a boathouse as a utilitarian building.
The collection of boathouses featured in the book
should challenge this view. See Drower, G. *House and
Garden*, March 1990, pp. 54-8. George Drower wrote
an excellent article on Victorian boathouses on the
Thames, in which he describes a selection of Thames
boathouses. It has been possible, with further
research, to classify the stylistic types of boathouse
and to compare the Victorian genre with that of
today.
39 The Thames, from its source near Kemble in
Gloucestershire, down to Dorchester, is known as the
Isis. The River Thame meets the Isis at Dorchester,
and from that point it is known as the Thames.

Dickens's *Dictionary of the Thames* (1887, 1994) p. 114. Dickens suggests that the name Isis is a 'fanciful derivation...[which] has no foundation in actual fact'. Peel, J.H.B. Op.cit. pp. 123 & 25. Peel quotes Camden (who published Britannia in 1586) as saying that 'the name Thames, or Tamesis, is a compound formed by the meeting of the Tame and the Isis.' Isis was an Egyptian goddess of fertility. 'The name Isis came, not out of Egypt, but from the Celts, who used Is as the root of their word for water'.

40 Blomfield, R. (1908) *The Mistress Art*.

41 *The Architect's Record*, July 1891-July 1892, pp. 199-210.

42 *The Building News*, April 8th 1904. There are other examples in the *Building News* of boat club designs, which demonstrates the interest in the building type during the period. See for example *The Building News*, May 19th 1882, p. 615.

43 *The Building News*, February 14th 1908, p. 237.

44 Schneer, J. (2005) pp. 21 & 218. *The Thames - England's River*.

45 Ibid. p. 288.

46 The term backwater is used in the book to indicate an area of water connected to the river, but away from the main stream.

Chapter 4 : The 1900s

47 Read, S. (ed.1989) pp.vi & viii, *The Thames of Henry Taunt*.

48 Bailey, P. (1987) pp. 84 & 57, *Leisure and Class in Victorian England*.

49 Pearall, R. (1973) p. 282, *Edwardian Life and Leisure*. E. Hobsbawm (1987, 1997) pp.46-55, *The Age of Empire* 1875-1914. The historian Eric Hobsbawm notes that 'from the middle of the 1890s until the Great War' the global economy was vibrant, but that there was an actual 'slowing-down in growth and a decline in the British economy'; the price of real wages actually fell from 1899-1913. The importance of the city of London as 'the switchboard for the world's international business transactions' promoting the 'invisibles' such as banking, insurance cannot be under estimated. The 'transformation in the market for consumer goods', with the ensuing rise of mass production also played a vital part in the economy at the time.

50 Webb, B, (1900) p. 195, *Our Partnership*.

51 Thompson, P. (1975, 1992) p. 44, *The Edwardians*.

52 Baldwin, J. (1994) p. 26, *Henley Heritage*.

53 Jerome K. Jerome. (1889, 2003) p. 153. *Three Men in a Boat*.

54 Pevsner, N. (1960, 1994) p. 257-8, *The Buildings of England, Buckinghamshire*. Curl. J.S. Op.cit. p. 198.

55 J. Mordaunt Crook, (1999) p. 220, *The Rise of the Nouveaux Riches*.

56 Bailey, P. Op.cit. pp. 6 & 124.

57 Ibid. p. 4.

58 Ibid. pp. 60- 61.

59 Burstall, P. (1981) p. 145, *The Golden Age of the Thames*. Burstall writes that Reading Rowing Club

dates from 1867, Maidenhead in the 1870s and that Cookham was 'growing' by 1884.

60 Leyland, J. (c.1897) p. 152, *The Thames Illustrated*.

61 Ibid. p.154.

62 *The Pictorial Record Special Edition for Reading*, c. 1900s. Berkshire Record Office.

63 Masterman, C.F.G. (1909) p. 158, *The Condition of England*.

64 Hattersley, R. (2004, 2006) pp. 266, 315-6 & 3, *The Edwardians*.

65 There are various sources for the history of lock building. Baldwin, J. Op.cit. p. 24. Baldwin writes that the 'first modern lock on the Thames was built at Swift Ditch, near Abingdon, in 1630' and that Humphrey Gainsborough, brother of the painter Thomas 'planned and supervised the construction of locks from Sonning to Hambleden' in the late eighteenth century. Belloc, H. Op.cit. p. 29, Hilaire Belloc confirms that the locks were invented 'as late as the sixteenth century.' Peel, J.H.B. Op.cit. pp. 29-30. Peel describes how Leonardo de Vinci (1452-1519) invented the lock 'for the Mortescara Canal, which supplied Milan with water'. The first English lock, he claims, was on the Exeter Canal in 1563. Most of the present locks on the Thames were built in the nineteenth century by the Thames Conservancy Board.

Chapter 5 : Lechlade to Oxford

66 Belloc, Op.cit. p. 32. Belloc is useful in his translation of place names on the Thames. Most, he writes, are of Saxon derivation, ford meaning a 'passage' or a 'going', thus Oxford can be translated as the 'ford of the droves' - presumably of oxen, and Wallingford could be described as a 'walled or embattled ford'. Ham and Hythe are of Teutonic derivation, ham meaning 'place' and Hythe a 'wharf or stage'. Incidentally above Lechlade the river becomes virtually un-navigable by boat, with a draught of 2' or more.

67 Ibid. pp. 14 & 24.

68 Ibid. p. 8.

69 Schneer, J. Op.cit. p. 169. The description 'Baby Thames' is taken from a letter written by William Morris.

Chapter 6 : Oxford to Reading

70 *The Oxford Chronicle*, 4.6. 1913 tells the story of the suffragettes destroying Rough's Boathouse at Long Bridges. K. Bradley's MA dissertation (1993) p.54, *The Suffrage Movement in Oxford* 1870-1920 also describes how 'the timber wharf near Folly Bridge [presumably this was Salter's] was extensively burnt' also by the suffragettes.

71 Leyland, J. Op.cit. p. 271.

72 Rowntree, D. *The Architectural Review*, no. 120, July-December 1956, pp. 37-42.

73 Judith Curthoys, 12.4.2006.

74 *Jackson's Oxford Journal (JOJ)*, 15th January 1881. p. 5.

75 Read, S. Op.cit. p. 49.

76 UC: E/H1/C2/1/no. 7. Charles Faulkner (1833-1892) was a 'university teacher and associate of William Morris'. He was 'appointed tutor in philosophy in 1857, he became praelector in mathematics a few years later' and was 'an active member of both college and university'. 'At the same time, though Faulkner led another life. As an undergraduate he played host to a collection of Birmingham students who met each evening in his rooms at Pembroke. Calling themselves the Set, and later the Brotherhood, this group included Edward Burne-Jones, William Fulford, R.W. Dixon and...William Morris'. 'He... accompanied William Morris on his tours of France in 1857 and 1858. When Morris joined Dante Gabriel Rossetti and others to paint the interior of the debating chamber of the Oxford Union Society (now the library) in 1857, Faulkner gave up his afternoons to help....This artistic experience was repeated when he helped decorate Morris's Red House at Upon, near Bexleyheath, Kent in 1859'. William Whyte, 'Faulkner, Charles Joseph (1833-1892)', *Dictionary of National Biography*, online edition – October 2005, Oxford.

77 Op.cit. UC: E/H1/C2/1 nos. 6 & 7.

78 The letter is dated April 17th 1880.

79 UC: EB4/51/6, July 24th 1880. The Reverend Sherwood writes that the boathouse 'was burnt almost immediately and rebuilt the next year'. *Oxford Rowing*, (1900) p. 95. A newspaper article makes clear that the building was unfinished at the time of the fire, which was believed to have been started accidentally by plumbers. *JOJ*, 15th January 1881, p. 5.

80 The blue toned brick has been darkened by an anti-vandalism paint.

81 Read. S. (ed.) Op. cit. p. 49.

82 A 1932 Ordnance Survey map (composite) shows three boathouses in the Nuneham area, one at Nuneham Court, one at Nuneham Park and the other above the lock.

83 Boyd, A.K. *The History of Radley College* 1847-1947 – Appendix on Rowing, The Reverend V. Hope.

84 Nuneham House itself was built in 1756 for Lord Harcourt. Harrison, I. (2004) p. 67 *The Thames From Source to Sea*.

85 Stephen Salter Junior (b. 1861) son of Stephen Salter (1825-1896). The younger Salter lived in Oxford and on the Isle of Wight. He started his artistic career in John Ruskin's Drawing School at Oxford and was later articled to F. Codd, the Oxford City Surveyor. *Who's Who in Architecture* (1914) p. 104, lists Salter as having designed, amongst other buildings, Lloyds Bank at Carfax Corner, Oxford, houses in Pangbourne and works for The Right Honourable Lord Harcourt, including many riverside residences. His speciality was 'old English domestic architecture'.

86 Belloc, H. Op.cit. pp. 64 & 77.

87 *Abingdon School Boathouse*, 2003. The earlier boathouse was built of steel with asbestos, and

leaked badly.

88 Timber Design Ltd, press release, 2003.

89 The 1932 O.S. map shows one boathouse at the lock.

90 See page 158.

91 Loudon, J. (1833, 1846, 2000) pp. 98-99, *The Encylopaedia of Cottage, Farm and Villa Architecture and Furniture*.

92 Pevsner, N. and Sherwood, J. (1974, 1996 edition) p.586, *The Buildings of England, Oxfordshire*.

93 The 1910 Ordnance Survey Map of Berkshire shows two boathouses at Shillingford Bridge, one before and one after the bridge.

94 The 1910 OS Map shows a boathouse above Benson Lock.

95 Beasley, D. (2004) *Wallingford - The Twentieth Century*.

96 The English Baroque employed classical motifs: the obelisk, the column, the pediment and the dome in a sensuous but still serious manner. The proportions appeared correct and conveyed architectural gravitas. The Edwardians became more frivolous with these attributes, their domes diminished to mere discs, their consoles were aggrandised, their orders assumed proportions previously undreamed of. A different kind of exuberance crept in, which would have been inappropriate to the seventeenth and eighteenth century Baroque. The 'Isomer' boathouse, further down the Thames, near Reading is another fine example of the Edwardian Baroque.

97 *Salter's Guide to the Thames*, Op.cit. p. 54. The church of St. Leonard's, Wallingford has an altar painting by G. D. Leslie. RA.

98 Leslie, G.D. (1888) p.155, *Our River*.

99 *Salter's Guide to the Thames*, Op. cit. p.54.

100 A modern pyramid shaped art gallery with a further boathouse below stands close to the old boathouse. The art gallery is a listed building, as is the synagogue on the site.

101 Read, S. (ed.) Op.cit. p. 81.

102 Drower, G. *House and Garden*, Op.cit.

103 Cariad is the original early spelling for the name.

104 *Salter's Guide to the Thames*, Op.cit. p.56.

105 Pevsner, N. and Sherwood, J. (1974, 1996) Op.cit. pp. 613-4.

106 *Salter's Guide to the Thames*, Op.cit. p.57.

107 Leyland, J. Op. cit. pp. 196-9.

108 Eade, B. (2002) p. 48, *Forgotten Thames*.

109 Farr, J.E. (2000) p.18, *Gatehampton - An Oxfordshire Hamlet*.

110 *The Building News*, September 2nd 1892, p. 315. The architect W. Ravenscroft FSA FRIBA (1848-?) also built the Masonic Buildings at Henley on Thames and Streatley Village Hall in 1898. He was a senior partner in the firm Ravenscroft, Son and Morris of Reading. Their work includes domestic buildings, Sunday Schools, churches and halls in the Thames' valley, at Goring and Pangbourne, a building at Wellington College, Berkshire, and also The University College, Reading. *RIBA Biographical File* and *Who's Who in*

Architecture (1914) p. 183.

111 Willcox, J. (1992) p. 52. For the photograph see *Pangbourne, An Illustrated History*.

112 Ibid. p. 53.

113 Jerome K. Jerome, Op. cit. p. 231.

114 Willcox, J. Op.cit. p. 68.

115 *Salter's Guide to the Thames*, Op.cit. p. 62.

116 Leslie, G.D. Op.cit. p. 140.

117 Read, S. (ed.) Op.cit. p. 99.

118 *Salter's Guide to the Thames*, Op.cit. p. 67

119 Read, S. (ed.) Op.cit. p. 101.

120 Rose, W. 'The boat builder Charles J. Talbot 1870?-1890s built barges, houseboats, landing stages etc at Algoa Wharfe, Caversham Bridge'.

121 For more information see *Salter's Guide to the Thames*. Also Burstall, Op.cit. p. 135. Burstall mentions three commercial boathouses in the area: J. Keel at Tilehurst, Moss' Boathouse, near Reading Rowing Club and A.H. East above Caversham Lock.

122 Burstall, Op.cit. p. 135.

Chapter 7 : Reading to Windsor

123 Jerome K. Jerome, Op.cit. p. 168.

124 Ibid.

125 Pevsner, N. and Sherwood, J. (1974, 1996) Op.cit. pp. 756-7. Stamp, G and Goulancourt, A. (1986) p.78, *The English House* 1860-1914. Ernest George was 'best known for his domestic buildings in the Queen Anne manner'. He won the RA Gold medal for architecture in 1859, the RIBA Gold Medal in 1890 and was President of the RIBA 1908-10. He was a brilliant water colourist, who was renowned for his sketches. The architect Guy Dawber wrote ' His houses invariably possess a sense of a home...they seemed always to fit the site, to grow out of the ground and his great artistic sense enabled him to see them as a completed whole whilst he was planning them.' His many pupils included Lutyens, Herbert Baker, Arthur Blomfield, Arnold Mitchell, S. D. Adshead and G. Schultz Weir. *The Builder*, November 15th 1922, p. 903.

126 Ordnance Survey Map 1932. This also shows a boathouse to the Mill House at Shiplake Lock.

127 Drower, G. *House and Garden*, Op.cit.

128 The Royal Institute of British Architects (RIBA) Drawings Collection at the V&A, ref: PA146/7(1-15).

129 The East Boat Building Company also had premises at the mouth of the Kennet.

130 *Salter's Guide to the Thames*, Op.cit. p.72.

131 Peel, Op.cit. p. 82. This tradition has apparently never been checked. The Lodden, being a tributary, has not been included in this book. There is an early boathouse on its banks, which has been carefully restored.

132 Read, S. (ed.) Op.cit. p. 119 and Curl, J.S. Op.cit. p. 91. A bressumer beam is a horizontal beam or plate over 'an opening in an external wall'; it can also refer, as it does in this case, to an area 'set forward from the lower part of the building to support an entire jettied wall in timber-framed construction'.

133 Curl, J.S. Op.cit. p. 411. A mascaron is 'a

representation of a human or partly human face, more or less caricatured, used as an architectural ornament'.

134 Pevsner, N. (1966, 1993) p. 192-3, *The Buildings of England - Berkshire*.

135 *The Guide to Henley*, (1826).

136 Leyland, J. Op.cit. p.171.

137 Drower, G. *House and Garden*, Op.cit.

138 Other awards given to the Henley Royal Regatta Headquarters include the 1987 Financial Times Architecture at Work Award for Industrial and Commerical Buildings, the 1988 Civic Trust Award for Outstanding Contribution to the Quality and Appearance of the Environment and a design award in 1994 from Wokingham District Council.

139 Classical architecture is defined by the use of the column and entablature. In their simplest form the column is categorised into five orders: Tuscan, Roman Doric, Roman Ionic, Roman Corinthian and Composite. A pediment is a triangular gable over a portico or facade, a cornice is a projecting horizontal moulding at the top of a building or a wall and a dentil is a 'small block forming one of a long horizontal series' set close under the cornice. See Curl, J.S. Op.cit. pp. 172 & 196.

140 In classical language a Venetian or Serlian window is a 'tripartite window...consisting of a central opening with a semicircular arch over it...supported by two columns or pilasters flanking narrower flat topped openings on either side'. Curl, J.S. Op.cit. p. 606.

141 *The Architectural Record*, no. 174, July-December 1986, pp.118-122.

142 Belloc, H. Op.cit. p. 121. Henley's first bridge was built in the thirteenth century.

143 Pevsner, N. (1974, 1996) Op.cit. p. 645.

144 No 26 Thameside, currently Harrington's Hairdressers, was the boathouse for the Henley Rowing Club.

145 Burnell, R. and Page, G. (1997) pp. 17, 21, 58, 62, 69, 70 & 200. *The Brilliants - A History of Leander Club*.

146 Pevsner, N. (1974, 1996). Op.cit. p. 640

147 Ibid. p. 639. Pevsner writes that Sir Frank Crisp probably designed Friar Park with the help of the architect M. Clarke Edwards.

148 Drower, G. *House and Garden*, Op.cit.

149 Read, S. (ed.) Op.cit. p. 117. It is also in *Salter's Guide to the Thames*, Op.cit. p. 80.

150 Leyland shows a photograph of a long rustic boathouse at the weir. Leyland, J. Op.cit. p. 163.

151 Leslie, G.D. Op.cit. p. 82.

152 Ibid. p. 77.

153 Leyland, J. Op.cit. p.148

154 Danesfield auction documents for the house, dated 13/6/1895. See also the 1926 Ordnance Survey map of the area.

155 Blomfield entered his uncle, Sir Arthur Blomfield's, London practice in 1881. Amongst other buildings he designed The Talbot Building at Lady Margaret Hall Oxford (1910-15), the former United Universities Club

(1906), the Regent Street Quadrant and part of Piccadilly Circus (1910-23). As an architectural theorist he wrote extensively on the Renaissance and the Edwardian 'Wrennaissance' revival. *The Mistress Art* (1908) called for architecture to be considered an art, based on the classical orders, which 'beautifies and enobles building construction'. Curl, J.S. Op.cit. p. 78 and *Building Design*, February 8th 1985, pp. 24-27.
156 *Country Life* 16 July 1927, pp. 90-94 and July 21 1928, pp. 81-85.
157 Kearley, H. (c.1930) *The Travelled Road*, Chapter XVII.
158 Ibid.
159 Listed building description SU 88 SW 8/154. The boathouse is Grade II listed.
160 Kearley, H. Op. cit Chapter XVII.
161 Jerome K. Jerome Op.cit. p. 152.
162 An ogee is an 'upright double curve, concave at the top and convex at the bottom.' Curl, J.S. Op.cit. p. 460.
163 Read, S. (ed.) Op.cit. p. 129. Belloc, H. Op.cit. p. 81. Belloc describes this as a 'Cell of Westminster'.
164 Read, S. (ed.) Op.cit. p. 129.
165 Peel, Op.cit. p. 69.
166 Leslie, G.D. Op.cit. p. 76.
167 Mansfield, K. *Waterfront*, 'Peter Freebody's Boathouse', November 2002, pp. 58-9.
168 Leslie, G.D. Op.cit. p. 75.
169 Eade, B. Op.cit. p. 65.
170 Read, S. (ed.) Op.cit. p. 116.
171 Buckinghamshire Record Office – Photographic Collection, Box 3, MAR 650, Francis Frith no. 23678.
172 See also *Salter's Guide to the Thames*, Op.cit. p.80.
173 Rose, W. 'One of the partnership of Meakes and Redknap was a boat-builder and the other a coffin-maker'.
174 *Records of Marlow Rowing Club* 1871-1921, Davis, A. Marlow 1921, pp.12-13.
175 This was replaced by the current suspension bridge by William Tierney Clark in 1829-31. He later built the suspension bridge over the Danube in Budapest. His daughter was christened Suspensiana, in deference to his passion.
176 Pevsner, N. (1960, 1994) Op.cit. p. 461.
177 De Maré, E. (1952) p. 115, *Time on the Thames*. De Maré was closely associated with The Architectural Press and published over twenty books on photography. *The RIBA Journal* (1999) p. 130, suggests that he was greatly acclaimed for 'broadening the perception of where architecture was to be found'.
178 *The Architect and Building News*, August 19th 1932, pp. 226-7.
179 On the early use of concrete David Yeoman writes that 'Weaver's Mill Swansea was the first reinforced concrete building to be put up in Britain'. Yeomans, D. (1997) p. 105, *Construction Since 1900 – Materials*. Alan Powers notes that the 'first fruits' of the Modernism [were] the Silver End houses in Essex' in 1927. Powers, A. (2007) p. 29, *Britain – modern architectures in history*.

180 Listed Building Description SU 8775586895. *The Architect and Building News* August 19th 1932, pp. 223-7.
181 Leyland, J. Op.cit. p. 124.
182 V. and A. Harvey, (1984) *Bright Images*, Bourne End, Bucks.
183 Eade, B. Op.cit. p. 69
184 Peel, R.H.B. Op. cit. p.57.
185 Read, S. (ed.) Op.cit. p. 143.
186 Drower, G. *House and Garden*, Op.cit.
187 Listed building description, The Boathouse, Cliveden Road, Cliveden SU 98 SW 7/2: SU9089384656. Curl. J.S. Op.cit. p. 198. George Devey promoted the 'Domestic Revival in the use of vernacular elements in his buildings. His first commission was at Penshurst, Kent where he designed cottages and various estate buildings from 1850 in a C15 style'.
188 Jerome K. Jerome, Op.cit. p. 78.
189 Burstall, P. Op.cit. p.56 & 137. Burstall uses the term 'lock-loungers'. Burstall also writes that H. Woodhouse provided boats at Maidenhead and 'in 1899 he built a very large boathouse and dressing-rooms...above Boulters'. Andrews and Wilders provided similar facilities at Maidenhead.
190 Leslie, G.D. Op.cit. p. 67.
191 See page 158 for further information on the Swiss chalet.
192 See *Salter's Guide to the Thames* p.80 for the location of the commercial boathouses.
193 *Kelly's Directory, Berkshire, Buckinghamshire and Oxfordshire*, (1899) pp. 110-111.
194 Ellis, G. (1902) p. 342, *Modern Practical Joinery*.
195 Leslie, G. D. Op.cit. p. 58.
196 Read, S. (ed.) Op.cit. pp. 146-7.
197 Maidenhead Rowing Club was established in 1876; the original building was constructed of timber with a corrugated iron roof. Maidenhead Rowing Club, 2007.
198 Read, S. (ed.) Op.cit. p.153.
199 Byrne, L.S.R. (ed.) (1933, 3rd edition) *Eton Boating Book* 1816-1932.
200 Ibid p. xxvii-xix.
201 Ibid pp. xx-xxv, *Eton College Boat House Committee Meetings* 1910-60, and 1934 Plan.
202 *Salter's Guide to the Thames*, Op.cit. p. 110.
203 Roberts, J. Op.cit. p. 151.
204 Listed building description 40380.
205 Curl, J.S. Op.cit. p.665. Curl writes that his masterpiece was St Stephen's (1868-71) Rosslyn Hill Hampstead; he also designed St Mary's in Ealing (1866-71) and St John the Baptist in Huntley (1861-3) Gloucestershire. His great houses include Tortworth Court in Gloucestershire (1849-52) and Shadwell Park, Norfolk (1856-60).

Chapter 8 : Walton Bridge to Richmond

206 Read S. (ed.) Op.cit. pp. 172 & 180.
207 For further commercial boatyards on this stretch see *Salter's Guide to the Thames*.
208 Eade, B. Op.cit. p. 85

209 Ellis, B. (2002) p. 17. *Walton Past*.
210 Tough, H. (c.mid-1980s) *The Geographical Factors Determining the Distribution of Boat-Builders on the Thames from Chiswick to Chertsey* 1850-1950. London Borough of Richmond upon Thames. See also *Salter's Guide to the Thames*, Op.cit. p.112.
211 Listed building description TQ1114168750.
212 Listed building description TQ1486969069.
213 *The Building News*, April 11 1890, p. 512.
214 Read, S. (ed.) Op.cit. p. 201.
215 Curl, Op.cit. p. 575. The Victorian art critic Ruskin favoured 'structural polychromy' featuring colour in material and decoration, both of which are seen in this boathouse.
216 Pargetting was common in England during the late Tudor period. It was produced by pressing moulds onto wet plaster to create a pattern.
217 Ordnance Survey Maps 1894 and 1915 for Kingston upon Thames.
218 Read, S. (ed.) Op.cit. p. 202.
219 Keith Wicks writes: 'The boathouses on the upper tidal Thames were generally of two types, wet boathouses and deep-water boathouses. Wet boathouses had a sloping slipway into which the high tide flowed twice per day. Part of the slipway generally remained dry for storage of...boats out of the water, whilst others would float up and down with the tide. In deep-water boathouses it was normal for some water to remain in the boathouse throughout most of the tidal range...Access to boats was usually along floating pontoons.'
220 Richmond Local Studies. Simpson, D. (1993) *Twickenham Past*, pp. 29-30.
221 Keith Wicks writes that this is the Poulett Lodge Boathouse, known locally as Thames Eyot Boathouse. Poulett Lodge now longer exists, but the ornate stone balustrade which fronted the building still stands and culminates at the boathouse.
222 To count the numerous boathouses of the late nineteenth century on the Thames using photographic, cartographic and literary evidence would probably prove inaccurate. Studies have confirmed that the commercial boathouse has rapidly declined since the early twentieth century.

Conclusion

223 *Building Design*, January 11th 2008, pp. 10-11.
224 De Botton, Op.cit. p. 155.

Bibliography

Arkkitehti 2002 & Turner Brooks Architects.

Belloc, H. (1907, 1998) *The Historic Thames*: Devon.

Blomfield, R. (1908) *The Mistress Art*: London.

Bailey, P. (1987) *Leisure and Class in Victorian England*: Toronto.

Baldwin, J. (1994) *Henley Heritage*: Henley-on-Thames.

Boldt Castle Yacht House, Thousand Islands, Canada.

Burstall, P. (1981) *The Golden Age of the Thames*: Newton Abbott.

Beasley, D. (2004) *Wallingford The Twentieth Century*: Gloucestershire.

Bradley, K. (1993) M.A. Dissertation, *The Suffrage Movement in Oxford* 1870-1920, Oxford Polytechnic.

Burnell, R. & Page, G. (1997) *The Brilliants A History of Leander Club*: GB

Building Design, 1985 & 1999.

Byre, L.S.R. (ed. (1933, 3rd edition) *Eton Boating Book* 1816-1932: London.

Christie, A. (1956, 2005) *Poirot – The Complete Ariadne Oliver, Dead Man's Folly*: London.

Curl, J. S. (1999) *Oxford Dictionary of Architecture*: Oxford.

Country Life 1927, 1928, 1966, 1996 & 2006.

Dickens Dictionary of the Thames, (1887, 1994): Devon.

Dewey, J. & S. & Beasley, D. (1989) *Window on Wallingford* 1837-1914: Wallingford.

Davey, P. (1980) *Arts and Crafts Architecture*: London.

Davis, A. (1921) *Records of Marlow Rowing Club* 1871-1921: Marlow.

De Botton, A. (2006) *The Architecture of Happiness*: London.

De Maré, E. (1952) *Time on the Thames*: London.

De Visser, J. & Ross. J. (2006) *Boathouses*: USA.

Dylan Thomas Archives, Carmarthenshire County Council.

Drower, G. (1990) *House and Garden* 'A boat's abode'.

Eade, B. (2002) *Forgotten Thames*: Gloucestershire.

Ellis, B. (2003) *Walton Past:* Sussex.

Farr, J. E. (2000) *Gatehampton – An Oxfordshire Hamlet*: Oxfordshire.

Fellows, R. (1985) *Sir Reginald Blomfield: An Edwardian Architect*: London.

Gray, A. S. (1985) *Edwardian Architecture*: London.

Hobsbawm, E. (1987, 1997) *The Age of Empire* (1875-1914): GB.

Hattersley, R. (2004, 2006) *The Edwardians*: London.

Harrison, I. (2004) *The Thames from Source To Sea*: London.

Harvey, V. & A. (1984) *Bright Images – The Story of the Upper Thames Sailing Club*: Oxfordshire.

Icon 2004.

International Marine Floatation Systems Archives & Swindler's Cove Boathouse.

Jerome, K. J. (1889, 2003) *Three Men in a Boat*: London.

Kearley, H. (c.1930s) *The Travelled Road*. Private Publication.

Kelly's Directory 1895 & 1899, Maidenhead, Berks, Bucks and South Oxon.

Kippo News 2005.

Leyland, J. (c.1897) *The Thames Illustrated*: London.

Leslie, G.D. (1888) *Our River*: London.

Listed Building Descriptions: English Heritage.

Loudon, J. (1833, 1846 & 2000) *The Encyclopaedia of Cottage, Farm and Villa Architecture and Furniture*: Bath.

Mordaunt Crook, J. (1999) *The Rise of the Nouveau Riches*: London.

Masterman, C.F.G. (1909) *The Condition of England*: London.

Mansfield, K. *Watercraft*, November-December 2002, 'Peter Freebody's Boathouse'.

Mills, J. Hesling, H. and MacLeman M. & K. (1996) *Rosehaugh – A House of its Time*: Inverness.

Musson, J. *Country Life,* August 1996, 'Temples to Boating'.

Ordnance Survey Maps - Berkshire: 1876, 1899, 1910, 1912-14, 1923, 1926, 1932 & 1938 Buckinghamshire - Kingston upon Thames - 1894 & 1915.

Mott, G. & Sample, A.S. (1989) *Follies and Pleasure Pavilions*: London.

Peel, J.H.B. (1967) *Portrait of the Thames*: London.

Pearall, R. (1973) *Edwardian Life and Leisure*: Newton Abbott.

Pevsner, N. (1966, 1993) *The Buildings of England – Berkshire*: London.

Pevsner, N. and Williamson, E. (1960, 1994) *The Buildings of England – Buckinghamshire*: London.

Pevsner, N. and Sherwood, J. (1974, 1996) *The Buildings of England – Oxfordshire*: London.

Powers, A. (2007) *Britain – modern architectures in history*: London.

Read, S. (ed. 1989) *The Thames of Henry Taunt*: Bristol.

RIBA Biographical Files: W. Ravenscroft FRIBA, Sir Reginald Blomfield FRIBA & Cecil James Parker, William Wood & Partners.

Roberts, J. (1997) *Royal Landscape – The Gardens and Parks of Windsor*: New Haven and London.

Ruskin, J. (1880, 1989) *The Seven Lamps of Architecture*: New York.

Salters Guide to the Thames (1914, Sixteenth edition): Oxford.

Schildt, G. (2007) *Alvar Aalto – His Life*: Finland.

Schneer, J. (2005) *The Thames England's River*: London.

Service, A. (ed. 1975) *Edwardian Architecture and Its Origins*: Hampshire.

Simpson, D. (1993) *Twickenham Past*: GB.

Sherwood, The Reverend W.E. (1900) *Oxford Rowing*: Oxford.

Stamp, G. & Goulancourt, A. (1986) *The English House* 1860-1914: GB

Thacker, F.S. (1914, 1968) *The Thames Highway*: Newton Abbott.

The Architect 1882.

The Architect and Building News 1932.

The Architect's Record 1891-1892.

The Architect's Journal 1994.

The Building News 1890, 1892, 1904, 1907 & 1908.

The Architectural Review 1956.

The Architectural Record 1986.

The Builder 1922.

The Directory of British Architects 1834-1914. (1993, 2001) British Architectural Library, RIBA: London.

The National Library of Australia – Rex Nan Kivell Collection.

The National Trust – Greenway Boathouse, 2007.

The Royal National Lifeboat Institution, Aldeburgh.

Thompson, P. (1975, 1992) *The Edwardians*: England.

Tough, H. (1980s) *The Geographical Factors Determining The Distribution of Boat Builders on the Thames From Chiswick to Chertsey* 1850-1950. Unpublished Dissertation. Richmond Local Studies.

University College, Oxford, Boathouse Archives.

Webb, B. (1948) *Our Partnership*: London.

Willcox, J. (1992) *Pangbourne, An Illustrated History*: Gloucestershire.

Worsley, G. (2004) *The British Stable*: New Haven and London.

Wyatt, J. *The Boater*, (2004-5) 'History of the Thames' Boatyards.'

Yeomans, D. (1997) *Construction Since 1900 – Materials*: London.

Boathouse Directory

Belsize Architects
48 Parkhill Road London NW3 2YP UK
mail@belsizearchitects.com

PLOT Architects
now JDS Architects and BIG Bjarke Ingels Group
JDS Architects Vesterbrogade 69d 1620 Copenhagen V DK
press@jdsarchitects.com
www.jdsarchitects.com
BIG - Bjarke Ingels Group
Norrebrogade 66d Z.sal DK-2200 Copenhagen N
press@big.dk www.big.dk

Turner Brooks
319 Peck Street New Haven Connecticut 06513 USA
turner@turnerbrooksarchitect.com

Boston Building Consultants
332 Congress Street, Ste 301, Boston MA 02210
617 542 3933

Tuke Manton Architects
20 Prescott Place London SW4 6BT UK
info@tukemanton.co.uk

Peter Freebody Thames Boathouses,
Mill Lane, Hurley, Berkshire SL6 5ND UK
peterfreebody@btconnect.com

KME Germany
AG Klosterstrasse 29 49074 Osnabr ü ck Germany
info-tecu@kme.com

Armand Le Gardeur
7 West 22nd Street, 3rd Floor, New York 10010
info@alegarch.com
www.alegarch.com

International Marine Floatation Systems IMFS 9365
River Road Delta Vancouver B.C. Canada VAG 1B4
info@floatinghomes.com

The Timber Frame Company
The Framing Yard 7 Broadway Charlton Adam Street
Somerset TA11 7BB
info@thetimberframe.co.uk
www.thetimberframe.co.uk

Sarah Wigglesworth Architects
9-10 Stock Orchard Street, London N7 9RW
mail@swarch.co.uk. www.swarch.co.uk

Thamesis Design and Construction Ltd
Riverstudio, Ray Mill Island
Boulters Lock, Maidenhead
Berkshire SL6 8PE
ian.burley@btinternet.com

Acknowledgements

The idea of a book on boathouses re-emerged every time I took a boat trip on the Thames. Long discussions with my friend and printmaker Katy Clemson, and my editor Hugh Tempest-Radford, brought it to fruition. My husband's patient driving of *Constant*, our tug, documenting the Thames was invaluable. Others have offered their advice, knowledge and encouragement. I am particularly grateful to Diana Cook and Richard Way of Way's Bookshop in Henley for their reading and comments, and to the many architectural practices and owners who have been generous in giving their photographs, or helping me obtain them. My debt is to Hugh Tempest-Radford, for having the temerity to publish, and for his encouragement and wise advice.

I am grateful to the following for their information: Sue Keane, Antonina Ivasenko, Konrad Ragnarsson, Andrew Cusack, Neil Koven, Ken Watson, John de Visser, Robert Down, Rosehaugh Estate, Lavinia Gibbs, Julian Blackwell, John McDonnell, Richard Norton, Dr Jonathan Price, Norman Guiver, Tony Money, Jock Mullard, John Short, David Beasley, Paul Conroy, Steve Royle, David Beck, John Calvert, Anthony Hudson, L. Stevens, Jeremy Paxton, Mrs A. Adams, Peter Delaney (Wargrave History Society), Jack Wyatt, Peter Symons, Mr and Mrs W. Rose, Mrs E. Bell, Mrs. V. Hill, Alan Pontin, S. Hayward-Jones, Tony Hobbs, Andy Trotman, Richard Goddard, Daniel Grist (Secretary Henley Royal Regatta) Michael Jones, Henley Management College, Brian Miller (Danesfield Hotel), Nigel Law, Roz Bond, Peter Hunt, Michael Davis, Madeleine Steele, Mrs Green, Slyvia Rutter, Patrick Walmsley, Vic Lundberg, David Brown (Lauristons Teddington), Mike Turk, Peter Wells, Kim Wilkie and Keith and Sylvia Wicks.

Every effort has been made to contact owners and photographers and to provide correct attributions.
Any inadvertent errors or omissions will be corrected in subsequent editions of this book.

Abbreviations
RIBA Royal Institute of British Architects
NTPL National Trust Picture Library
RNLI Royal National Lifeboat Institution
NMR National Monuments Record
OUBC Oxford University Boat Club

Index

Page numbers in *italics* refer to captions.

River Thames
From Source to Richmond

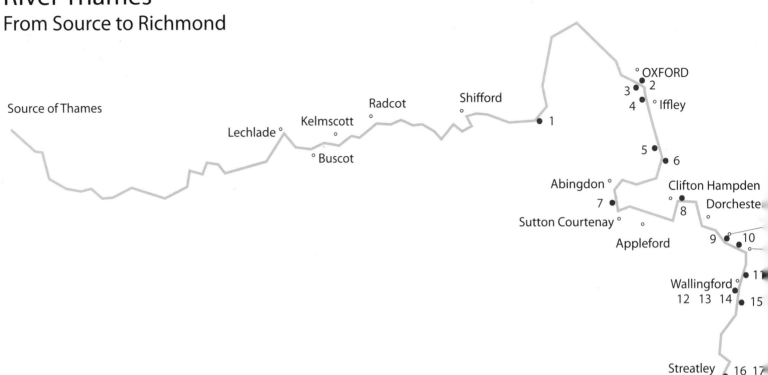

Source of Thames

OXFORD
Iffley
Lechlade
Kelmscott
Radcot
Shifford
Buscot
Abingdon
Clifton Hampden
Dorcheste
Sutton Courtenay
Appleford
Wallingford
Streatley
Gorin
Basildon
Pangbour

Key to Illustrated Boathouses

1 Rustic	11 Howbery	21 The Shanty	31 Red Lion
2 College Boathouses	12 Neo-Baroque	22 Isomer	32 Wharfe Lane Boathouses
3 University College	13 OUBC	23 Balihoo	33 Water's Edge
4 Isis	14 Agatha Christie's	24 Cape Cod	34 Hambleden
5 Radley College	15 Carmel College	25 Carport and Balcony	35 Wittington
6 Nuneham Courtney	16 Cariad and Howgate	26 Val Wyatt's	36 Lady Place
7 Abingdon School	17 Nun's Acre	27 Park Place	37 Aqua
8 Clifton Hampden	18 Saunders	28 Hybrid	38 Old Bridge
9 Shillingford Court	19 Coombe Park	29 Marsh Mill	39 Thames Lawn
10 Shillingford Bridge	20 Old Swan	30 Henley Royal Regatta	40 Rippling Water